THE MANUAL OF LEARNING STYLES
by
Peter Honey and Alan Mumford

Table of Contents

The Manual of Learning Styles was first published in November 1982. The second edition in 1986 included a revised version of the questionnaire and the descriptions of styles. These changes simplified the language and removed most of the colloquialisms. No further changes of this kind have been made in this third edition but the text of the Manual has been substantially rewritten.

Published and distributed by Peter Honey,
Ardingly House,
10 Linden Avenue,
Maidenhead,
Berkshire, SL6 6HB

ISBN 0 9508444 7 0

CHAPTER 1

SETTING THE SCENE FOR LEARNING STYLES

This Manual is for all trainers, educators and development advisers - in fact for anyone who has an interest in helping people learn. (For convenience we will use the term trainer throughout this Manual.) As in previous editions the focus is on learning styles; what they are, how they can be identified and how they help to make learning more effective.

There are two ways in which to use the Learning Styles Questionnaire. Firstly, at the back of the Manual you will find master copies of the Learning Styles Questionnaire, descriptions of the styles and two different versions of the score key. These are available for unlimited photocopying.

Secondly, you may well have purchased the software package of the Learning Styles Questionnaire which is now available for IBM PCs and 100% compatible machines. If so, you will find included within this package a disk of the Learning Styles Questionnaire and a pamphlet providing you with all the information necessary to run the system. Read the accompanying licence agreement before opening the envelope which contains the disk.

Learning is such a fundamental process that many people take it for granted, conveniently assuming that by the time they are adults they have learned how to learn and need no further assistance with the process. Thus lecturers concentrate on lecturing and assume students are skilled at such learning activities as listening, note taking, researching, essay writing and revising. Trainers too often assume that learners are empty buckets waiting to be filled up by the training method the trainer favours. The fact that the buckets are different sizes, and/or leak and/or are upside down is conveniently overlooked.

Yet it is patently clear that people vary not just in their learning skills but also in their learning styles. Why otherwise might two people, matched for age, intelligence and need, exposed to the **same** learning opportunity react so differently? One person emerges enthusiastic, able to articulate and implement what has been learned. The other claims it was a waste of time and that nothing has been learned. The question we all face is why, with other factors apparently constant, one person learns and the other does not? This Manual aims to show that the reason for the divergence stems from unspoken preferences about how to learn. Perhaps the learning opportunity involved 'having a go' by being pitched in at 'the deep end' with minimal guidance. It so happened that this suited one person's style but not the other who preferred to learn by being given some information and ideas on how to act before 'having a go'.

The term learning styles is used as a description of the attitudes and behaviours which determine an individual's preferred way of learning.

Most people are unaware of their learning style preferences. They just know vaguely that they feel more comfortable with, and learn more from, some activities than others. Trainers often realise people learn differently, but may not be sure how and why. In this Manual we show how learning styles can be identified and how this can help both trainer and learner.

The case for helping people to be more effective learners ought to be self evident, yet many trainers still give insufficient recognition to it. It is perhaps **the** most important of **all** the life skills since the way in which people learn affects everything else. We live in the post industrial 'information' age where data have a shorter shelf-life and where transformational changes are less predictable and occur more rapidly than ever before. Clearly learning is the key, not just to surviving but to thriving on all these changes. So this Manual gives help on the crucial issue of learning to learn, thus enabling people to continue to learn long after an event which a trainer has designed.

What is learning?

Learning has happened when people can demonstrate that they know something they didn't know before (insights and realisations as well as facts) and/or when they can do something they couldn't do before (skills). We learn in two substantially different ways. Sometimes we are 'taught' through formal structured activities such as lectures, case studies and books. We also learn from our experiences, often in an unconscious, ill defined way. Learning dedicated to the acquisition of knowledge is both more familiar and more straightforward than experiential learning. It is more familiar not because we necessarily do it more often, but because most people associate the word 'learning' with the acquisition of facts rather more than with the messier process of learning from day to day experiences. As we shall see, learning style preferences have implications for **all** types of learning.

The range of influences on learning

The history of the development of ways to help people learn how to be more effective is relatively short; perhaps fifty years in the UK and a little longer in the USA. One of the constant features in that history has been the discovery of a succession of what were claimed to be uniquely appropriate 'methods'. Lectures were abandoned and replaced by case studies. Books about human relations techniques were replaced by T Groups. Structured training need analyses gave way to individual commitment to self development. The problem of ineffective learning remains, because all these 'solutions' dealt too exclusively with teaching methods and not with differences in individual approaches to learning.

This Manual is about the contribution which can be made to effective learning by an understanding and use of individual styles of learning. We are, however, clear that we are describing one of several major aspects which must be 'right' before effective learning occurs. We are not adding another innovation and claiming that without it nothing useful will be done; we are saying that with attention to individual learning styles, much more effective learning can take place.

In order to emphasise the importance of placing learning styles in the total learning context, it is worth remembering the large number of factors which influence the extent of learning. The following diagram shows just some of the many influences on what is learned or not learned.

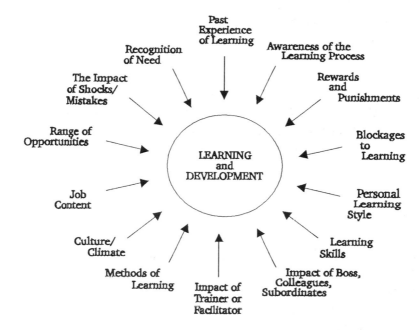

This helps to put this Manual into its proper perspective since it can be seen that it focuses on just one of the range of influences; personal learning style. However, the learning cycle and learning styles are particularly important for the trainer because they fall within an area that the trainer can directly influence.

Learning as a continuous process

Learning is a life-long process. It never makes sense to say we have learned all there is to learn or that our learning is complete.

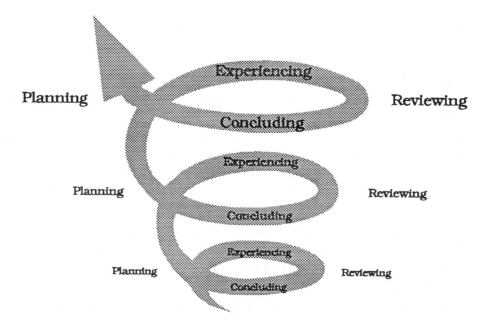

The continuous process is rather like the coils in a spring or, as Professor John Morris has described it, a never-ending spiral. Each coil of the spring or loop in the spiral has four distinct stages on each cycle.

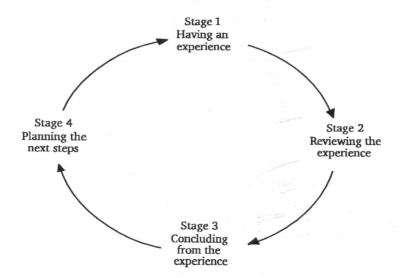

Our description of the stages in the learning cycle originated from the work of David Kolb (see references). Kolb uses different words to describe the stages of the cycle and four learning styles. The similarities between his model and ours are greater than the differences. However, since we first published the Learning Styles Questionnaire in 1982 many users have found it enjoys a greater face validity with learners mainly because, unlike Kolb, we refrain from asking direct questions about how people learn. We based it instead on what managers and professional people do.

A learner can start anywhere on the cycle because each stage feeds into the next. A person could for example, start at stage 2 by acquiring some information and pondering it before reaching some conclusions, stage 3, and deciding how to apply it, stage 4. On the other hand someone could start at stage 4 with a technique that they plan to incorporate into their *modus operandi*. Using the technique would then be at stage 1 in the cycle before reviewing how it worked out, stage 2, reaching conclusions stage 3, and modifying the technique in the light of the experience, stage 4.

This continuous, iterative process is so fundamental that it underpins many other approaches. The scientific method is one example. Many problem solving/decision making processes also map onto the stages in the learning cycle as do the methods of continuous improvement in Total Quality Management.

Ways of distorting the learning cycle

The four stages, experiencing, reviewing, concluding and planning are mutually supportive. None is fully effective as a learning procedure on its own. Each stage plays an equally important part in the total process (though the time spent on each may vary considerably).

Most people, however, develop preferences which give them a liking for certain stages over others. The preferences lead to a distortion of the learning process so that greater emphasis is placed on some stages to the detriment of others. Here are some typical examples:-

–   Preferences for experiencing such that people develop an addiction for activities to the extent that they cannot sit still but have to be rushing around constantly on the go. This results in plenty of experiences and the assumption that having experiences is synonymous with learning from them.

–   Preferences for reviewing such that people shy away from first hand experiences and postpone reaching conclusions for as long as possible whilst more data are gathered. This results in an 'analysis to paralysis' tendency with plenty of pondering but little action.

–   Preferences for concluding such that people have a compulsion to reach an answer quickly. This results in a tendency to jump to conclusions by circumventing the review stage, where uncertainty and ambiguity are higher. Conclusions, even if they are the wrong ones, are comforting things to have.

–   Preferences for seizing on an expedient course of action and implementing it with inadequate analysis. This results in a tendency to go for 'quick fixes' by overemphasising the planning and experiencing stages to the detriment of reviewing and concluding.

Learning styles

Learning styles are the key to understanding these different preferences. Learning styles, in common with any other style, have in themselves been learned as people repeated strategies and tactics that were found to be successful and discontinued those that were not. In this way preferences for certain behaviour patterns develop and become habitual. These styles tend to be strengthened as people gravitate towards careers that are compatible with their preferred modus operandi.

Here are paragraphs describing four learning styles. (The same descriptions are repeated on a one-page handout to make photocopying easy.)

Activists

Activists involve themselves fully and without bias in new experiences. They enjoy the here and now and are happy to be dominated by immediate experiences. They are open-minded, not sceptical, and this tends to make them enthusiastic about anything new. Their philosophy is: "*I'll try anything once*". They tend to act first and consider the consequences afterwards. Their days are filled with activity. They tackle problems by brainstorming. As soon as the excitement from one activity has died down they are busy looking for the next. They tend to thrive on the challenge of new experiences but are bored with implementation and longer term consolidation. They are gregarious people constantly involving themselves with others but, in doing so, they seek to centre all activities around themselves.

Reflectors

Reflectors like to stand back to ponder experiences and observe them from many different perspectives. They collect data, both first hand and from others, and prefer to think about it thoroughly before coming to any conclusion. The thorough collection and analysis of data about experiences and events is what counts so they tend to postpone reaching definitive conclusions for as long as possible. Their philosophy is to be cautious. They are thoughtful people who like to consider all possible angles and implications before making a move. They prefer to take a back seat in meetings and discussions. They enjoy observing other people in action. They listen to others and get the drift of the discussion before making their own points. They tend to adopt a low profile and have a slightly distant, tolerant, unruffled air about them. When they act it is part of a wide picture which includes the past as well as the present and others' observations as well as their own.

Theorists

Theorists adapt and integrate observations into complex but logically sound theories. They think problems through in a vertical, step by step, logical way. They assimilate disparate facts into coherent theories. They tend to be perfectionists who won't rest easy until things are tidy and fit into a rational scheme. They like to analyse and synthesise. They are keen on basic assumptions, principles, theories, models and systems thinking. Their philosophy prizes rationality and logic. *"If it's logical it's good"*. Questions they frequently ask are; *"Does it make sense?" "How does this fit with that?" "What are the basic assumptions?"* They tend to be detached, analytical and dedicated to rational objectivity rather than anything subjective or ambiguous. Their approach to problems is consistently logical. This is their 'mental set' and they rigidly reject anything that doesn't fit with it. They prefer to maximise certainty and feel uncomfortable with subjective judgements, lateral thinking and anything flippant.

Pragmatists

Pragmatists are keen on trying out ideas, theories and techniques to see if they work in practice. They positively search out new ideas and take the first opportunity to experiment with applications. They are the sort of people who return from management courses brimming with new ideas that they want to try out in practice. They like to get on with things and act quickly and confidently on ideas that attract them. They tend to be impatient with ruminating and open-ended discussions. They are essentially practical, down to earth people who like making practical decisions and solving problems. They respond to problems and opportunities 'as a challenge'. Their philosophy is: *"There is always a better way"* and *"If it works it's good"*.

Each style 'connects' with a stage on the continuous learning cycle. People with Activist preferences, with their 'I'll try anything once' approach, are well equipped for Experiencing. People with Reflector preferences, with their predilection for mulling over data, are well equipped for Reviewing. People with Theorist preferences, with their need to tidy up and have 'answers', are well equipped for Concluding. Finally, people with Pragmatist preferences, with their liking for things practical, are well equipped for Planning. The diagram below shows the learning styles positioned around the learning cycle.

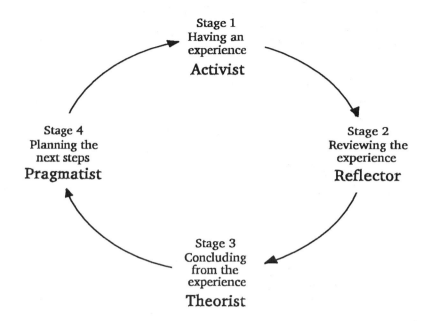

This Manual

This Manual, the third edition, is again practical rather than theoretical. After ten years' experience by ourselves and others, it shows that learning activities can be designed to encompass the full cycle. We can also confirm that people are helped to be more effective learners if they are aware of their learning style preferences. The questionnaire results provide a starting point, not a finishing point because knowledge of learning styles is only useful if it is applied rather than merely recorded. In the chapters that follow we describe how this can be done. The most significant uses explored in this Manual are:-

–   Increased awareness of learning activities which are congruent or incongruent with a person's dominant style(s).

–   A better choice by trainers and learners of those activities, leading to more effective and more economical learning provision. Avoidance of inappropriate learning experience is both good in itself and less likely to lead to the Shakespeare effect, where inappropriate early experiences put young people off for life.

–   An identification of ways in which a person's less effective learning processes and skills can be improved.

–   Advice on how the different learning styles of trainers, learners, bosses and subordinates influence the way they help others to learn.

This edition of the Manual improves on earlier editions in a variety of ways amongst them being:-

–   Fuller descriptions of how to introduce, administer, score and interpret the Learning Styles Questionnaire.

–   Expanded examples of how to use learning styles to design programmes and learning to learn sessions.

–   More 'norms' for additional occupational groups and updated norms calculated from a data base which has expanded over a ten year period.

–   A more comprehensive bibliography of books, articles and papers on learning styles.

CHAPTER 2

ADMINISTERING SCORING AND INTERPRETING THE LEARNING STYLES QUESTIONNAIRE

A master copy of the Learning Styles Questionnaire together with two versions of the score key (why two will be explained later in this chapter) is included with this Manual with permission to photocopy ad infinitum.

The Learning Styles Questionnaire

The questionnaire probes people's learning style preferences by asking 80 questions; 20 for each of the four styles. Since there are no right or wrong answers, the questionnaire invites people to respond to each item honestly. (Our experience is that people do respond honestly if they are assured the questionnaire is being used for development not for assessment or selection.) People work through the questionnaire rapidly, between ten and fifteen minutes is typical, weighing the extent each item applies to them. Items that are 'agreed' are ticked; items that are 'disagreed' arc crossed. People are encouraged to respond to all 80 items however marginal some of their ticks/crosses.

Scoring and interpreting the questionnaire

Scoring the questionnaire has been kept as straightforward as possible. The score key 'unscrambles' the items and lists those that probe Activist tendencies, Reflector tendencies and so on. People are asked to indicate the items they ticked ie agreed more than they disagreed, and total the number of ticks in each column. This results in 'raw' scores, each out of a maximum of 20, for the four learning styles.

Raw scores whilst they give an indication of where a person is on a scale of zero, ie no items ticked, to 20, ie all items ticked, are in themselves not very meaningful. Our approach has been to establish 'norms' with which individual scores can be compared. Norms result from analysing the actual scores of people who have completed the questionnaire. The norms are calculated by dividing the scores into five bands:-

A   the point at which 10% of the scores are above and 90% are below.

B   the point at which 30% of the scores are above and 70% are below.

C   the middle 40% of scores with 20% above and 20% below the mean.

D   the point at which 70% of the scores are above and 30% are below.

E   the point at which 90% of the scores are above and 10% are below.

Each of the five bands of scores arrived at in this way is indicative of a person's learning style preferences:-

–   Any scores in the A band indicate a very strong preference since statistically only 10% of the scores fall into this band.

–   Scores in the B band indicate strong, but not very strong, preferences.

–   Scores in the C band indicate moderate preferences.

–   Scores in the D band indicate low preferences.

–   Scores in the E band indicate very low preferences since statistically 90% of the scores are above this band.

When the scores for well over one thousand people were divided into these bands in 1982 the following norms resulted:-

	Very strong preference	Strong preference	Moderate preference	Low preference	Very low preference
Activist	13-20	11-12	7-10 (mean 9.3)	4-6	0-3
Reflector	18-20	15-17	12-14 (mean 13.6)	9-11	0-8
Theorist	16-20	14-15	11-13 (mean 12.5)	8-10	0-7
Pragmatist	17-20	15-16	12-14 (mean 13.7)	9-11	0-8

These are referred to as the general norms because they are based on such a large population of scores. Interestingly, calculations with data collected since 1982 have confirmed the accuracy of the general norms, even though the population upon which they are based has now risen to 3,500. The general norms are published in a panel on one version of the score key to make it easy for a person to convert their four raw scores into the bands indicating preferences.

To give an illustration of how the bands affect the interpretation of the results, let us suppose the raw scores for an individual are Activist 11, Reflector 11, Theorist 11, Pragmatist 11. We have chosen these scores because they admirably illustrate the importance of using the norms to reach an interpretation rather than jumping to a conclusion based on the raw scores alone. If you plot the raw scores onto a questionnaire profile based on the general norms the following picture emerges:-

Profile based on general norms for 3,500 people

Activist	Reflector	Theorist	Pragmatist	
20, 19, 18, 17, 16, 15, 14, 13	20, 19, 18	20, 19, 18, 17, 16	20, 19, 18, 17	Very strong preference
12, (11)	17, 16, 15	15, 14	16, 15	Strong preference
10, 9, 8, 7	14, 13, 12	13, 12, (11)	14, 13, 12	Moderate preference
6, 5, 4	(11), 10, 9	10, 9, 8	(11), 10, 9	Low preference
3, 2, 1, 0	8, 7, 6, 5, 4, 3, 2, 1, 0	7, 6, 5, 4, 3, 2, 1, 0	8, 7, 6, 5, 4, 3, 2, 1, 0	Very low preference

According to the general norms therefore, this person has a strong preference for Activist, a moderate preference for Theorist and low preferences for Reflector and Pragmatist.

Whilst the general norms are convenient, norms vary for different occupational groups and a comparison with an appropriate group may give a different interpretation. The second score key made available with this Manual allows for this by not including the table based on the general norms. Instead, it invites people to plot their raw scores on the arms of a cross and consult the norms for an appropriate group in order to reach an interpretation. Norms for various groups are given in chapter 9 of this Manual and at the end of section 1 in the sister booklet 'Using Your Learning Styles'. If you wish to establish norms for your organisation and/or for different occupational groups these can be calculated for you. This service is explained in chapter 9.

Here are some examples to illustrate how the interpretation might change depending on whether general norms or other norms are used. Let us continue with the example used earlier where the four raw scores were 11-11-11-11. Applying the general norms resulted in the following interpretation.

Style	Raw score	Interpretation
Activist	11	Strong preference
Reflector	11	Low preference
Theorist	11	Moderate preference
Pragmatist	11	Low preference

If we now apply the norms for three different occupational groups to these raw scores the interpretations change.

First, the norms for 189 Salespersons

	Band A	Band B	Band C	Band D	Band E
Activist	17-20	15-16	12-14 (mean 13.3)	9-11	0-8
Reflector	15-20	12-14	10-11 (mean 11.5)	7-9	0-6
Theorist	17-20	14-16	9-13 (mean 11.4)	6-8	0-5
Pragmatist	18-20	16-17	13-15 (mean 14.1)	10-12	0-9

If we plot the point at which these norms start to indicate a strong preference on the arms of the cross on the score key ie Activist 15, Reflector 12, Theorist 14, Pragmatist 16 using a dotted line and then plot the four scores of 11, 11, 11, 11 a different interpretation emerges.

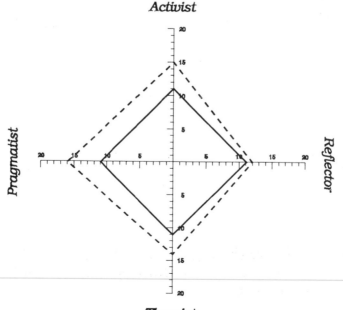

All four raw scores fall inside the dotted line so none of them are strong. Whereas against general norms an Activist score of 11 is strong, in comparison with a sales population it is low. The results are now:-

Style	Raw score	Interpretation
Activist	11	Low preference
Reflector	11	Moderate preference
Theorist	11	Moderate preference
Pragmatist	11	Low preference

Second, the norms for 178 Production Managers

	Band A	Band B	Band C	Band D	Band E
Activist	12-20	9-11	6-8 (mean 7.4)	3-5	0-2
Reflector	17-20	15-16	11-14 (mean 12.7)	7-10	0-6
Theorist	19-20	17-18	14-16 (mean 15.2)	12-13	0-11
Pragmatist	19-20	17-18	15-16 (mean 16.0)	12-14	0-11

This time the dotted lines on the diagram below show the points at which strong preferences begin for Production Managers, ie Activist 9, Reflector 15, Theorist and Pragmatist 17.

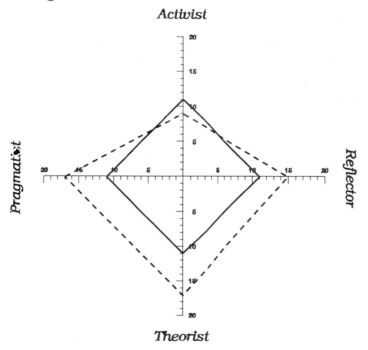

This time the score for Activist goes outside the dotted line indicating a strong preference for a Production Manager but, as we have seen, a low preference for a sales person.

The results are now:-

Style	Raw score	Interpretation
Activist	11	Strong preference
Reflector	11	Moderate preference
Theorist	11	Very low preference
Pragmatist	11	Very low preference

Third, the norms for 160 Finance Managers

	Band A	Band B	Band C	Band D	Band E
Activist	10-20	8-9	6-7 (mean 7.0)	3-5	0-2
Reflector	19-20	16-18	14-15 (mean 14.9)	10-13	0-9
Theorist	18-20	16-17	13-15 (mean 14.5)	11-12	0-10
Pragmatist	18-20	16-17	14-15 (mean 15.3)	11-13	0-10

Now the dotted line represents the point at which strong preferences begin for Finance Managers ie Activist 8, Reflector, Theorist and Pragmatist 16.

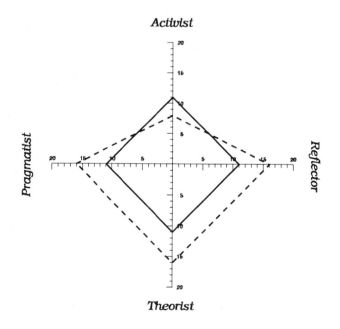

The results are now:-

Style	Raw score	Interpretation
Activist	11	Very strong preference
Reflector	11	Low preference
Theorist	11	Low preference
Pragmatist	11	Low preference

As these examples show, the interpretations vary depending on the norms applied to the raw scores. For most purposes the general norms will suffice. Occupational norms are useful when you have a homogeneous group eg of salespeople rather than a multi-occupational group. Using the more specific norms helps you understand the reality of the group you are working with, and enhances their acceptance of the questionnaire results.

An example of how to introduce and administer the questionnaire to a group

Before using the questionnaire with others it is vital that trainers complete it themselves and thoroughly understand how it is scored and interpreted.

Here is an illustration of how to introduce, administer, score and interpret the questionnaire in a one and a half hour session with a group embarking on a learning experience together such as a course or workshop. (Alternative ideas are given in chapter 7.) Of course the questionnaire can also be administered on a one to one basis as part, say, of a counselling session or before putting together a tailor-made development plan.

1. Start with some general scene setting remarks but avoid, at this stage, getting into any details about the learning cycle or learning styles. For example you could say *"As we all realise, we are here to learn from the various experiences built into this programme. It would be easy to assume that we all know how to learn and are already efficient learners from experience. It is also tempting to assume that we all learn in identical ways. Let us start by checking out both assumptions. This short questionnaire has been designed to reveal learning style preferences which you have probably developed quite unwittingly over a period of time. The questionnaire only takes ten minutes or so to complete. After you have done it I will say more about the styles it is designed to probe and let you score your own questionnaire and get a quick result. The questionnaire is entirely for your development, not for assessment/selection."*

2. Distribute the questionnaire and check that people have understood the few lines of introduction at the top of the first page. Whilst people work though the questionnaire, circulate unobtrusively to make sure that all items are ticked or crossed and to get a feel for whether the members of the group are roughly synchronised in their speed of response. Leave people to complete the questionnaire at their own pace. Activists will tend to finish it faster than Reflectors!

3. When everyone in the group has finished, and **before** getting them to score the questionnaire, run through the following points.

    There are two kinds of learning:-

    –   acquiring data in order (hopefully) to be able to use them to do something

–   acquiring data **as a result** of doing something.

Both kinds of learning are necessary and entirely complementary.

After leaving formal education we all spend significantly more time learning by a process of trial and error than we do by listening to 'teachers' or reading.

Learning from **any** activity should be a continuous process. Show the continuous learning cycle with four stages on each circuit (see page 4 in chapter 1).

It is rare for anyone to be equally 'comfortable' with each of these stages. Most people have learning style preferences that predispose them to overemphasise some stages and underemphasise others. Give the 'analysis to paralysis' and 'quick fix' examples (see pages 4-5 in chapter 1).

4.   Distribute the handout describing the four learning styles of Activist, Reflector, Theorist and Pragmatist. Give people time to read it and suggest that as they do so they might like to underline the words/phrases/sentences they recognise as being typical of them. Assure them that they will probably find bits and pieces typical of themselves in different paragraphs.

5.   Show how the learning styles connect with different stages on the continuous learning cycle

   –   Activist with having experiences

   –   Reflector with reviewing

   –   Theorist with concluding

   –   Pragmatist with planning.

6.   Distribute the score key. If you want the group to use the general norms, use the score key that provides the table giving the different weightings for each style. If you want your group to use other norms, for a particular occupational group perhaps, have the appropriate norms ready and use the version of the score key that provides the arms of a cross with no built in norms.

7.   Call on each person in turn to indicate their preferences. Record these on a flip chart so that the group can see the trends that have emerged. It is best to 'code' the results:-

   vs   for very strong preferences
   s   for strong preferences
   m   for moderate preferences
   l   for low preferences
   vl   for very low preferences.

It also helps to show up trends more clearly if you use different colours for example **vs** and **s** in green, **m** in blue and **l** and **vl** in red.

8.   Distribute copies of the 'Using Your Learning Styles' booklet. This short booklet is packed with practical ideas on what a person can do in the light of their learning style preferences. Perhaps the most immediately useful parts for someone who has just completed the questionnaire are:-

–   the norms for different groups

–   how to choose learning activities to suit your style.

–   how to strengthen an under utilized style.

Questions and Answers

Here are the questions that people most often ask about learning styles, the questionnaire and the results together with suggested answers.

Are there only four learning styles?

Four learning styles offer three worthwhile and practical advantages.

–   they are easy to remember

–   they reinforce the stages people need to go through in order to be balanced learners

–   they are widely understood, accepted and used by learners.

The four styles are a convenient way of describing differences in learning preferences and, of course, they map onto the stages on each loop of the continuous learning cycle. Some researchers have suggested that there are only two learning styles or orientations; doing and thinking. The doing orientation tends to overlap with a combination of Activist and Pragmatist. The thinking orientation overlaps with Reflector and Theorist.

Work on brain dominance also tends to the view that there are two styles; Right brain (intuitive, spontaneous, qualitative) and Left brain (factual, analytical and quantitative). Right brain dominance tends to overlap with a combination of Activist and Pragmatist. Left brain dominance overlaps with Reflector and Theorist. Interestingly and more recently, the brain has been divided into four thinking processes (upper and lower left and upper and lower right) so it's back to four again.

Can learning style preferences change?

Yes, learning styles, just like any other learned characteristics, are modifiable either at will or by a change of circumstances. Many people have deliberately set out to strengthen an underdeveloped style and thus become a more rounded learner. (The booklet 'Using Your Learning Styles' gives advice on how to do this.) Alternatively, when people change jobs and/or organisations, the altered influences have an affect on learning styles. Suppose, for example, someone moved from a 'quick fix' culture to an organisation that by the nature of its work was more reflective. The decrease in the speed of working and the emphasis placed on the painstaking collection and analysis of data would be likely to increase Reflector/Theorist **behaviour** and, over time, to affect the style preferences. It may well be that a person experiencing such a change would retain their 'first love' preferences for Pragmatist/Activist but being forced to use Reflector/Theorist would undoubtedly strengthen their presence in the person's repertoire.

Similarly, people moving from Sales to Marketing would be likely to find different occupational learning style preferences. For example, moderate Activists on Sales norms would be very strong Activists in a Marketing role (unless they deliberately tried to change).

Why do the questionnaire items probe general behavioural tendencies and not learning?

Since most people have never consciously considered **how** they learn, it is not helpful to ask questions that directly enquire into this. If you ask people how they learn prior to introducing them to the continuous learning cycle, they will simply say they 'just do' and are often incapable of articulating the process they go through. It is more useful, therefore, to ask people questions they can answer that are indirectly indicative of their preferred learning styles. To do so is certainly more helpful (there seems little point in asking people questions they can't answer) and enjoys greater face validity. The items in the questionnaire also admirably illustrate how learning style preferences underpin and are associated with everyday behavioural tendencies. This helps demonstrate the fundamental importance of learning styles.

How accurate are self-perceptions?

The accuracy of the perceptions is usually confirmed by people who know the individual in a work context or have shared experiences on a course. (Views of a domestic partner may differ, as some individuals behave differently at home.)

Sometimes a third party observer of someone's outward behaviour may conclude that the person had, say, Activist preferences. This is because people sometimes behave one way whilst feeling/thinking another way. Someone with Reflector preferences may, for example, behave like an Activist because that is expected of them and/or there is pressure to do so. Other people inevitably have to base their perceptions on the behaviour they observe. This may mislead them into concluding that behaviour is inevitably indicative of an underlying preference. When it comes to likes and dislikes, each individual is best qualified to answer.

This is not to deny that self-perceptions can be misleading. The answers are easy to fake if someone is determined to give a misleading impression. They are unlikely to do so if the assurance that the questionnaire is being used as an aid to development has been given.

Why does the questionnaire only allow binary choice, tick or cross?

To keep it simple. In the original research we tested a version of the questionnaire with a range of answers such as very frequently - frequently - sometimes - infrequently - never. It rendered the same preferences as the simpler version. We therefore decided to keep it simple and not unnecessarily to complicate the questionnaire. As a consequence some people feel uncomfortable with being forced to respond one way or the other but they are usually reassured when they understand that the questionnaire is designed to reveal four **general tendencies** and not a detailed analysis of their whole personality.

Why is the questionnaire so repetitious?

Because in probing preferences for four styles it offers twenty items for each style. The questionnaire never repeats a question but some of the close associations between items make it appear repetitious. In fact, research shows that the questionnaire could be shorter and still render valid data about people's learning style preferences. However, we kept it to twenty items per style because this gives people a fuller picture of what is involved in each style and gives them more choice when it comes to deciding which items to practise more deliberately.

Must all the questionnaire items be answered?

Yes, because if some items are left blank they might all fall within one learning style and therefore lead to an underestimate of that style.

What if people don't believe their results?

We suggest individuals do the following:-

1. Check that you still accept each tick/cross.

2. Re-examine items that were marginal to see if you have a propensity always to tick them or cross them. Decide again on these marginal choices, making sure that you balance your marginal choices. If you still find your choices have been predominantly ticks or crosses and the result is still not how you see yourself, try the next suggestion.

3. Collect feedback from other people's observations of you either on the course or back at work to see to what extent their perceptions match the questionnaire results. In our experience when this has been done the feedback tends to confirm the preferences indicated by the scores.

Aren't labels misleading/stereotyping?

Like any categorisation they are a convenient oversimplification. The styles have to be called **something**; the labels Activist, Reflector, Theorist and Pragmatist are shorthand. For both trainers and learners the labels are a starting point for discussion on how an individual learns. That discussion will remove any misleading judgements.

Responsibilities of trainer and learner

It will be seen that we strongly believe that the questionnaire should not be used solely as a secret 'design tool' by the trainer. The data should be shared. However there are different responsibilities:-

The trainer initially 'owns' the questionnaire results for:-

- recommending attendance at a particular kind of programme

- the overall design of a course or sections of it

- creating effective learning groups

- choosing roles within a programme to use or develop individual learning preferences

- using the results in encouraging learning to learn.

Learner and trainer together use the data for:-

- deciding between different kinds of learning opportunity eg whether to attend a particular course

- identifying particular kinds of learning opportunity on the job

- selecting activities within a programme.

The learner has primary responsibility for:-

- explicitly using the results of the questionnaire while planning or undertaking a learning activity on or off the job.

A tool for development, not selection

While there might be an obvious temptation to use the questionnaire as a selection tool, we have generally advised against this. To do so reduces the likelihood that people will complete the questionnaire with full honesty. In addition, there are no data to support reliability and validity for this purpose.

CHAPTER 3

LEARNING ACTIVITIES AND LEARNING STYLES

Introduction

We have shown in the previous chapter that there are differences in the predominant learning styles of individuals. We now go on to show that various learning activities can be assessed in terms of their relationship to learning styles. For the purpose of this chapter, we are assuming that the learning needs of the individual have been properly assessed and that the individual is committed to trying to meet them. Similarly, we are assuming that the learning activity, whether on or off the job, has been properly designed according to the best principles so that, seen purely as a learning activity, it is fully efficient. (See Binsted in the bibliography in chapter 10.) By efficient we mean that the method is appropriate to the need, eg the provision of practical work if you want to develop skill. Our concern here is to establish the difference between a learning activity which is efficient in general, and one which is effective for a particular individual.

The relationship of styles and learning activities

Just as some individuals are heavily dominated by one learning style, or are particularly weak in one style, so some learning activities are dominated by explicit or implicit assumptions about learning styles. The activity may be so geared to a particular style of learning as to cause a mismatch with any participant whose own major preferences are different. For example, major post experience programmes at the Business Schools tend to emphasise rationality, logic and system; values which are sought by Theorists. Some interactive skills programmes require people to learn largely through analytical reflection on experiences on the course, a process well suited to Reflectors. Generally courses are based on the learning styles of course runners not the learners.

Of course just as there are individuals whose learning styles are widely spread so there are learning activities which contain opportunities to learn in different styles. An example of this would be an interviewing course which involves role plays. Strongly Activist learners will enjoy playing roles; if, as is likely, they are also low Reflectors, they are likely to be uncomfortable and ineffective when asked to observe others role playing.

Our concern in that kind of situation is to establish how learners can be helped to respond to those aspects which are foreign to their preferred learning style.

In this chapter we look first at the kind of activities which are more, or less, congruent with each of the four styles. This gives help in some situations where an individual's learning needs have been determined and we are trying to think of activities which might meet those needs.

Then we turn the coin round the other way, to look at the circumstances where someone may have received details of a learning activity and is trying to assess for themselves, or others, the kind of learner for whom it might be appropriate.

Choosing activities related to styles

The activities which are most congruent with each of these styles are set out in the following lists. The lists are intended first to help guide people positively towards learning activities which they will find sympathetic. Learners may find that they can undertake the activities with a greater awareness of the potential for learning. Alternatively they may find that they are missing out on some activities which ought, from their basic style, to be attractive to them.

Secondly, the lists also identify activities which are much less compatible with a dominant style. In some cases the information may be used negatively - *"don't try this"* - but in other cases it may be possible to make the activity more acceptable despite its apparent incompatibility.

Activists

Activists learn best from activities where:-

- There are new experiences/problems/opportunities from which to learn.

- They can engross themselves in short 'here and now' activities such as business games, competitive teamwork tasks, role-playing exercises.

- There is excitement/drama/crisis and things chop and change with a range of diverse activities to tackle.

- They have a lot of the limelight/high visibility, ie they can 'chair' meetings, lead discussions, give presentations.

- They are allowed to generate ideas without constraints of policy or structure or feasibility.

- They are thrown in at the deep end with a task they think is difficult, ie when set a challenge with inadequate resources and adverse conditions.

- They are involved with other people, ie bouncing ideas off them, solving problems as part of a team.

- It is appropriate to 'have a go'.

Activists learn least from, and may react against, activities where:-

– Learning involves a passive role, ie listening to lectures, monologues, explanations, statements of how things should be done, reading, watching.

– They are asked to stand back and not be involved.

– They are required to assimilate, analyse and interpret lots of 'messy' data.

– They are required to engage in solitary work, ie reading, writing, thinking on their own.

– They are asked to assess beforehand what they will learn, and to appraise afterwards what they have learned.

– They are offered statements they see as 'theoretical', ie explanation of cause or background.

– They are asked to repeat essentially the same activity over and over again, ie when practising.

– They have precise instructions to follow with little room for manoeuvre.

– They are asked to do a thorough job, ie attend to detail, tie up loose ends, dot the is, and cross ts.

Reflectors

Reflectors learn best from activities where:-

– They are allowed or encouraged to watch/think/ponder over activities.

– They are able to stand back from events and listen/observe, ie observing a group at work, taking a back seat in a meeting, watching a film or video.

– They are allowed to think before acting, to assimilate before commenting, ie time to prepare, a chance to read in advance a brief giving background data.

– They can carry out some painstaking research, ie investigate, assemble information, probe to get to the bottom of things.

– They have the opportunity to review what has happened, what they have learned.

– They are asked to produce carefully considered analyses and reports.

- They are helped to exchange views with other people without danger, ie by prior agreement, within a structured learning experience.

- They can reach a decision in their own time without pressure and tight deadlines.

Reflectors learn least from, and may react against, activities where:-

- They are 'forced' into the limelight, ie to act as leader/chairperson, to role-play in front of on-lookers.

- They are involved in situations which require action without planning.

- They are pitched into doing something without warning ie to produce an instant reaction, to produce off-the-top-of-the-head ideas.

- They are given insufficient data on which to base a conclusion.

- They are given cut and dried instructions of how things should be done.

- They are worried by time pressures or rushed from one activity to another.

- In the interests of expediency they have to make short cuts or do a superficial job.

Theorists

Theorists learn best from activities where:-

- What is being offered is part of a system, model, concept, theory.

- They have time to explore methodically the associations and interrelationships between ideas, events and situations.

- They have the chance to question and probe the basic methodology, assumptions or logic behind something, ie by taking part in a question and answer session, by checking a paper for inconsistencies.

- They are intellectually stretched, ie by analysing a complex situation, being tested in a tutorial session, by teaching high calibre people who ask searching questions.

- They are in structured situations with a clear purpose.

- They can listen to or read about ideas and concepts that emphasise rationality or logic and are well argued/elegant/watertight.

- They can analyse and then generalise the reasons for success or failure.

- They are offered interesting ideas and concepts even though they are not immediately relevant.

- They are required to understand and participate in complex situations.

Theorists learn least from, and may react against, activities where:-

- They are pitchforked into doing something without a context or apparent purpose.

- They have to participate in situations emphasising emotions and feelings.

- They are involved in unstructured activities where ambiguity and uncertainty are high, ie with open-ended problems, or sensitivity training.

- They are asked to act or decide without a basis in policy, principle or concept.

- They are faced with a hotchpotch of alternative/contradictory techniques/methods without exploring any in depth, ie as on a 'once over lightly' course.

- They doubt that the subject matter is methodologically sound, ie where questionnaires haven't been validated, where there aren't any statistics to support an argument.

- They find the subject matter platitudinous, shallow or gimmicky.

- They feel themselves out of tune with other participants, ie when with lots of Activists or people of lower intellectual calibre.

Pragmatists

Pragmatists learn best from activities where:-

- There is an obvious link between the subject matter and a problem or opportunity on the job.

- They are shown techniques for doing things with obvious practical advantages, ie how to save time, how to make a good first impression, how to deal with awkward people.

- They have the chance to try out and practice techniques with coaching/feedback from a credible expert, ie someone who is successful and can do the techniques themselves.

–   They are exposed to a model they can emulate, ie a respected boss, a demonstration from someone with a proven track record, lots of examples/anecdotes, a film showing how its done.

–   They are given techniques currently applicable to their own job.

–   They are given immediate opportunities to implement what they have learned.

–   There is a high face validity in the learning activity, ie a good simulation, 'real' problems.

–   They can concentrate on practical issues, ie drawing up action plans with an obvious end product, suggesting short cuts, giving tips.

Pragmatists learn least from, and may react against, activities where:-

–   The learning is not related to an immediate need they recognise, ie they cannot see an immediate relevance/practical benefit.

–   Organisers of the learning, or the event itself, seems distant from reality ie 'ivory towered', all theory and general principles, pure 'chalk and talk'.

–   There is no practice or clear guidelines on how to do it.

–   They feel that people are going round in circles and not getting anywhere fast enough.

–   There are political, managerial or personal obstacles to implementation.

–   There is no apparent reward from the learning activity, ie more sales, shorter meetings, higher bonus, promotion.

Analysis of learning activities

Our activity lists have given indications of the kind of learning processes which will be more, or less, successful with particular learning styles. The lists are focused outward from the learners; they specify the kinds of activity which will be more likely to help learners with a particular style. However, many people may have to make a choice in the reverse situation, when the first problem is to assess a particular learning opportunity (usually a course) and see what kind of learning processes are involved. In this section we turn our attention to some examples of learning opportunities and test them to see what is said explicitly, or implied, which will help determine their likely congruence with one or more learning styles. Since course brochures do not identify the relationship between what they offer and learning styles, we give our interpretation.

As we have already said, some learning opportunities involve activities appropriate to more than one style; a learner may in those cases benefit from those aspects which he or she finds congruent but be turned off by processes which he or she dislikes. In contrast, some learning opportunities are so heavily dominated by one process that the likelihood is that only those learners with a largely congruent style will learn anything.

The cases given below are illustrative of the approach we recommend and are not a comprehensive survey of all possible learning opportunities. Our intention is to illustrate in sufficient depth and with a sufficient range of examples so that readers can pick up and use the approach themselves.

The cases about courses are anonymous in the sense that we do not quote the institutions involved. They are, however, real; all quotations are taken from descriptive material about an existing course. Our comments presume that the descriptions are a close approximation to the reality of the courses as designed by tutors and experienced by course members.

A major post experience management course

The brochure says:-

> "The programme has four major objectives around which the design has been formulated. It aims to:-
>
> Improve the manager's understanding of the economic, technical and social changes taking place in the environment and their implications for a company's operations.
>
> Increase the manager's capacity to analyse and resolve the important policy questions which face organisations in both the short and longer term.
>
> Improve knowledge and understanding of developments in the general and functional management processes which provide the necessary framework for managing in the face of change.
>
> Challenge the manager to understand and then reinforce or modify the attitudes which influence his or her behaviour in the complex multinational business settings of today."

The brochure also gives the following information about teaching methods, (Note, more than incidentally, that it talks about teaching methods, not learning methods.)

Teaching methods

> "Teaching methods vary since different subjects lend themselves to varying forms of presentation. Thus, whilst lectures can be used to present facts, or highlight general background information, case discussions put the necessity for creative analysis more forcibly on to participants, guided in their analysis and discussion by the faculty. In addition, seminars, small group discussions, projects and group presentations all play a role in the programme. Groups are also used as an individual's resource for projects and as a source of feedback on his own attitudes and behaviour.

Outside the classroom or seminar room, a substantial volume of reading is necessary to supplement and prepare for class sessions, and a great deal of valuable informal discussion with faculty, with other participants or with visiting speakers, takes place. The School possesses a first-class international management library which participants are encouraged to use".

Activists: The emphasis on the general environment, on case discussions and analysis, and on 'substantial volume of reading' and the lack of emphasis on 'here and now' activities suggest that Activists will not be happy with a lot of the course processes.

Reflectors: Reflectors would apparently have to define and make many of their own Reflector experiences on this course. There is no indication that the course is explicitly structured to meet at least half of their needs. While they will enjoy the opportunity to analyse case studies, some of their other characteristics might make the course a difficult experience. Reflectors, carrying out their listening/observing on a course not designed to aid that process explicitly, risk being seen as low contributors. They could be a good 'source of feedback' to others, but how effective will others be in providing feedback to them?

Theorists: The course description is strongly related to the Theorist's needs for systems, concepts, interrelationships of ideas and events and dealing with complexity. The statement of objectives would, in itself, be persuasive to Theorists, since it seems to be authoritative and well rounded.

Pragmatists: The general statements of objectives might not be fully persuasive to Pragmatists; the objectives would probably be insufficiently clearly related to their preferences for direct links to their jobs. Pragmatists would be more influenced by an examination of detailed course content, for which we do not have room here.

All these comments derive from the written material about the course. They should be tested against other evidence derived from visits or discussions with previous participants. Are the trainers really of the intellectual quality to attract Theorists or are they alternatively at the level of plausibility to attract Pragmatists? Is the course sufficiently geared to the immediate needs of Pragmatists in terms of easily transferable techniques? How far does the course, in practice, provide protected opportunities for Reflectors to review what they are learning and, if this is provided, what is done to prevent Activists from running away?

A marketing course

This is what the brochure says about programme content:

"The emphasis throughout the programme is on the integration of the various aspects of marketing into a coherent strategy, the co-ordination of marketing with other functions of the company, and the development of a symbiotic relationship between the company and its environment.

The opening segment of strategic marketing management provides the opportunity for participants to develop an in-depth understanding of the key concepts which provide the foundations for successful marketing strategies. Here we emphasise topics such as demand analysis and demand management, the marketing mix, product portfolio analysis, and market segmentation. In addition, the tools of financial analysis are introduced so that they can be used throughout the programme.

During the middle segment of the programme, participants choose between two sections. One relates to the marketing of consumer goods and services and the other covers the marketing of industrial goods and services. This specialisation enables each participant to study issues and situations of maximum relevance to his or her responsibilities.

In both sections, specific situations studied will include companies active in a wide range of products and services.

The final portion of the programme examines the development and evolution of the marketing strategy including the assessment of environmental changes, the analysis of competitive battles, and the management of strategy implementation.

Throughout the programme the emphasis is on rigorous analysis, careful strategy formulation, effective implementation, and meticulous monitoring and control."

Activists: Strongly Activist oriented learners would be as much antagonised by the brochure as Theorists might be encouraged! They might not get beyond the statement about the 'symbiotic relationship between the company and its environment'. However, Activists probably would not read the brochure carefully, if at all. If they went on a course, and the course was as described, they would be uncomfortable with rigorous analysis and meticulous monitoring and control. Activists would dislike the solitary work of reading cases, and would probably 'take a ride' on others who had done the reading, participating volubly but superficially.

Reflectors: The problem is again how far the course, which may suit them in giving them a chance to assimilate before commenting, offers them support for other aspects of their Reflector style. While the analysis of cases is congruent, is the 'hurly-burly' of debate, even in small groups, likely to suit them? How will they respond to being asked to present their analysis to a large group of managers?

Theorists: A course which emphasises strategy, co-ordination and the development of a symbiotic relationship will be attractive to Theorists. They will further be encouraged by the attention given to key concepts, and they will positively enjoy the opportunity to engage in 'rigorous analysis'.

Pragmatists: If the emphasis is too strongly on concepts and systems, particularly in the early stages of the programme, they may be less attracted than Theorists. However, the emphasis on particular topics and the choice of specialisation should help them. This latter point is particularly important in supporting the choice of this course for Pragmatists as compared to a course which did not offer the opportunity to study cases of more direct relevance. (Theorists would be much less bothered by the absence of directly applicable material.)

An Action Learning programme

Action Learning has become a generic title for a number of activities not all of which would be recognised or accepted by Reg Revans as being genuine examples of his major contribution. We base the following interpretations on what Revans himself has said.

Revans has said of Action Learning that it was designed: *"to help each manager observe more keenly his present condition, by obliging him to list (for his colleagues) his goals, the obstructions that bar those goals, the means by which he intends to remove those obstructions"*.

Action Learning is based on his view that behavioural change is more likely to follow the reinterpretation of past experience than from the acquisition of fresh knowledge. It is also based on an understanding of learning as a social process. In Action Learning learners are helped to learn from each other.

Revans has no time for traditional management education or educators; in his approach, the role of teachers is to contrive conditions in which managers may learn with and from each other. Crucially, Action Learning tackles real problems in real time in the real world. The problems are defined as a project and learners collect the data necessary to help them resolve the problem.

Activists: The sense of participating in something relatively new would be attractive to Activists, as would the emphasis on tackling real problems. However, they would be irked by the length of the project, by the necessity to get clarification of terms of reference, by attempts to provide regularity and structure and by the process of reviewing what has been learned. Activists might enjoy the project work; but they would dislike the 'set' discussion in which actions and learning are reviewed.

Reflectors: Reflectors would appreciate some major features, especially the opportunity to produce carefully considered analyses, the process of reviewing what has occurred within the project and within the learning group. They would enjoy the process of thinking things over, and the opportunity to give and receive feedback.

Theorists: Theorists are likely to be attracted to some elements of Action Learning and repelled by others. They will like the opportunity of being stretched by a complex problem. They will probably appreciate, without always committing themselves to, the theory behind Action Learning. They will probably however, increasingly find themselves uneasy about concentration on a particular project, and the possible absence of a process of generalisation. Whatever the care with which the initial structure of the exercise is set up, it is likely to move into conditions of ambiguity and uncertainty; conditions especially difficult for Theorists.

Pragmatists: The high face validity of tackling real problems, and the requirement to produce action plans, make this an attractive process for Pragmatists. This is especially true where people work on problems for which they are accountable in their own organisations. Consultancy projects in a different organisation may be less attractive.

An experience of being coached

Coaching is the process by which one person tries to guide another to improve their effectiveness. One example might be listening to a rehearsal of an important presentation and suggesting improvements; or going over a written report and highlighting ways in which it would better meet the interests of recipients. Coaching might be given by questioning, guidance or illustrative performance. It was proposed as a major and universal management need a few years ago. One of the reasons for the failure of this process to catch on widely was that it required managers to behave in ways which were unacceptable to them. Another reason was that no attention was paid to the learning style of the recipient. Differences in learning styles between the person giving, and the person receiving the coaching experience are likely to be crucial. (Chapter 6 illustrates the general point.)

Activists: Activists are unlikely to respond favourably to directive coaching where skill or knowledge is explained or demonstrated; they would dislike the passive element. Nor would they be more responsive to non-directive coaching, the more subtle form in which a coach attempts to get points across through questions which cause learners to review and learn from their own activities. Activists would be likely to see the approach as too analytical and long-winded if indeed they recognised what was happening at all.

Reflectors: The opportunity to watch someone else, or to review in a fairly well protected situation their own activities in response to questions would be welcomed by Reflectors. They would not respond so well to direct instruction 'do it this way', where they might want more evidence that it was the 'right' way. Also Reflectors would be unhappy if asked to 'perform' without some preparation.

Theorists: Theorists would probably respond well to a well prepared coaching situation whether directive or non-directive so long as the sessions were planned and not accidental. They would require the basis of the coaching to be intellectually respectable, eg not simply being given techniques but being given explanations of why they work. They would also need the chance to work out the value of the process rather than having to accept it from an authority figure (boss or teacher).

Pragmatists: Pragmatists are likely to be highly responsive to coaching, providing the subject matter has clear relevance to their own current performance, and providing the person offering the coaching is seen as authoritative. If the activity has high face validity the Pragmatists will participate in the process so eagerly that they may build on and improve what is being offered.

An experience of going along with John

The process of learning called 'sitting by Nellie' is still widely used. In the managerial setting it includes those occasions when a manager is given the opportunity to observe a more experienced colleague in action. We will take as an illustration a manager who attends a negotiation session with Trade Union representatives: she has no prime role but is attending because she will have the responsibility of negotiating at a later date. She is there to learn.

Before moving on to our analysis, you might like to pause and write down your own views on how each of Activist, Reflector, Theorist and Pragmatist might respond.

Activists: Activist learners would probably initially welcome the experience, especially if it was really novel and clearly related to a future role. Activists would be less attracted if they had experience previously of other negotiations. They would not be worried if the opportunity was given without warning. Their actual learning response, however, would be unlikely to be very effective. They would be unhappy about being on the sidelines and would not naturally think of ways in which to make use of the experience. Activists would have to be given considerable guidance and help to overcome their natural style.

Reflectors: This is a situation which Reflectors like and can make use of. They will make best use of it if given prior notice so that they can think over what they will try to get out of the session, and organise their observations. Reflectors would not need to discuss their observations with anyone else. They would not require a lot of help beforehand, but would probably be happy to use help.

Theorists: Theorists would benefit most if the session is carefully prepared, their own participation structured and if the existing company negotiator is, by the standards of the learner, highly competent. Theorists are less likely to benefit if thrown in without warning; they will want to know what the history is, what the strategy is, what in precise terms they can learn from the session. If, however, the situation was new, their intellectual curiosity might make even an unprepared session potentially acceptable.

Pragmatists: Given the requirement to be involved in future negotiations, Pragmatists would welcome the opportunity and would make effective use of either a planned or unplanned opportunity. They would respond favourably to planning the experience beforehand but would be unhappy if they were not given the chance to discuss the session afterwards.

A course using outdoor activities (called Adventure Training in the USA)

A three day leadership course for graduates, who had worked in an organisation for two years or so and were on the brink of becoming managers, was devised using outdoor activities as the main learning vehicle. The objectives for the course were to:-

- *recognise the contribution the leader makes to building and leading effective teams*

- *describe alternative leadership styles and identify own preferred leadership style*

- *choose a style appropriate to meet the leadership demands of different situations*

- *delegate tasks (even tedious and unpleasant ones) whilst maintaining/enhancing the motivation levels of people*

- *describe and recognise the features of a successful team*

- *describe the different roles necessary for successful teams and identify their own preferred role*

- *explain the links between what was learned and the role of the manager, set individual objectives and commit to specific plans to implement what has been learned back at work.*

Six exercises provided the outdoor challenges. Participants took it in turns to have a go at leading the team. Participants also completed a questionnaire designed to throw light on whether they tended to use a directive or collaborative style when leading. After each exercise the trainers led a review aimed at surfacing certain lessons.

Overall half the time on the course was spent carrying out the six exercises and half doing thorough reviews. (Unfortunately, many outdoor experiences do not give enough time to reviewing and concluding.)

Activists: Graduates with Activist preferences would be attracted to outdoor activities. They would enjoy the challenge of solving physical tasks. The more they were set 'mission impossible' and 'now get out of that' challenges the more engrossed they would become in succeeding. By contrast, the lengthy reviews of what had been learned would be tedious for Activists. In fact, the more they had enjoyed the outdoor activity the more impatient they would tend to be with the review periods.

Reflectors: Graduates with Reflector tendencies would shy away from opportunities to take the lead, preferring to observe or take lower profile roles within the team. They would, however, come into their own during review periods and be good at recalling the details of what had happened during the exercise.

Theorists: Graduates with Theorist preferences would be interested in the concepts associated with different leadership styles and the idea of achieving synergy in a team by an amalgam of different styles and roles. They would want to adopt a systematic approach to group working and to the way outdoor exercises were tackled. Theorist demands for order and structure would conflict with Activist preferences to do things on an intuitive spontaneous basis. Both would stand to learn much from each other in this classic left brain, right brain tussle if they were given review periods to work through the differences.

Pragmatists: Graduates with Pragmatist preferences would enjoy the outdoor exercises but be troubled about dissimilarities with 'normal' work activities. The more the connections between the exercises and back at work situations the happier Pragmatists would become about relevance. Pragmatists would tend to be good at planning approaches to the various exercises and at resolving what to do different/better back at work.

The key to planning a course using outdoor activities is to resist the temptation to pack it full of activities. It must be designed explicitly to take people round each stage in the learning cycle with balanced attention to each stage. Short activities are best, **always** followed by an opportunity to pause to review and conclude, **always** followed by an invitation to convert conclusions into plans ready for the next loop on the continuous learning cycle.

A multi-disciplinary project team

An organisation anxious to improve the quality of their customer care and stem customer attrition decided to set up a task force to investigate ways and means and produce recommendations. The members of the task force were drawn from a cross-section of the organisation's main functions - personnel, sales, finance, manufacturing and so on. This multi-disciplinary team was due to meet weekly for two half day sessions and produce recommendations within three months. The team's terms of reference were broad; 'to recommend the actions needed to significantly improve customer satisfaction'.

Activists: Team members with Activist preferences would start off full of enthusiasm for the project and see it as a challenge and a welcome diversion from their normal day to day responsibilities. However their initial enthusiasm is likely to fade once they get into the semantics of agreeing specific objectives for the project and the 'drudgery' of conducting surveys and other diagnostic activities. They would feel happier with opportunities to generate ideas if other team members also share their Activist tendencies.

Reflectors: Reflectors in the team would most enjoy the investigative phases of the project and become less happy as the deadline for producing recommendations approached. They might even call for an extension to enable them to gather more data and ponder different interpretations. Reflectors would also find it difficult to cope if the majority of team members were Pragmatists and Activists. In these circumstances Reflectors would be dragged along by the 'go for it' fraternity but harbour reservations about the wisdom of closing down the options too soon.

Theorists: Theorist team members would feel most unhappy with the ambiguous terms of reference for the project. They would press for something more specific to get a clearer vision of what success looked like. Theorists would also fret about how to measure increases in customer satisfaction and feel uneasy about the subjectivity of the concept. Once the ambiguity had been reduced and **if** the team settled down into a disciplined way of working, the Theorists in the team would become progressively happier and more productive.

Pragmatists: Team members with Pragmatist preferences would relish the opportunity to participate in a credible project with an important potential contribution to the organisation's future success. They would be keen to discover proven techniques for improving customer satisfaction - preferably by learning the tricks of the trade from other organisations who had a customer care track record.

Summary

We have shown in this chapter that, using our list of learning activities, it is possible to assess critically the content of various learning opportunities and see which learning styles are most likely to be well matched with them.

The actions we advocate are to:-

–   look at those learning activities which dominate within a style

–   assess the impact of these on identified learning needs

–   determine which activities are most likely to be effective for a particular kind of individual

–   review which learning style is likely to be involved in various kinds of learning opportunity

–   assess how this relates to the preferred style of an individual.

Of course, it may be possible (as well as desirable) to help individuals develop their weaker styles in order to take advantage of a wider range of opportunities. Chapters 5 and 7 show how this might be done.

CHAPTER 4

DESIGNING AN OFF-THE-JOB PROGRAMME

Despite the fact that people spend only a fraction of their working lives on courses, seminars, workshops and the like, such occasions have an important part to play in helping people to learn. This is because off-the-job programmes are unashamedly designed to promote learning. All those involved, providers and participants, are in no doubt that learning is the name of the game even if they have little idea what the rules are and how to play. This contrasts sharply with most working environments where achieving is top priority and there is a tacit assumption that people will learn as they go along. In a very real sense, therefore, an off-the-job programme is an ideal opportunity to create a temporary mini 'learning organisation'. Indeed there is no excuse since on a course there are far fewer variables to control than in the normal workplace.

Learning styles have many implications before, during and after a training programme and this chapter will explore some of these and show how to use the questionnaire during these different phases.

Using learning styles before a training programme

1. To help with the identification of training needs

The questionnaire can be used as part of a survey to identify training needs. We believe that information about the characteristic learning styles of any target population - be they apprentices, clerical trainees, graduates or managers - is always worth collecting and taking into account before designing a piece of training.

In a training needs analysis exercise where all the managers throughout the whole organisation were surveyed, the questionnaire was included. Prior to the questionnaire results being known, the company training manager had assumed that a fairly standard management skills course would fit the bill. Indeed he had even held preliminary discussions with a number of external training organisations and briefed them on the likely contents of the course. However, once the questionnaire results were known the training manager was persuaded to have second thoughts. In summary, the questionnaire results showed that the predominant learning style amongst managers in the company was Pragmatist. There were, however, important differences hierarchically. For example, the company directors and senior managers were by far the most Pragmatic, with Activist a strong back-up style. Middle and first level managers on the other hand had Theorist as their back-up style with Reflector next and Activist last.

These results indicated quite clearly that a tailor-made management development activity for this particular company needed to have the following ingredients to be accepted by, and useful for, the majority of managers.

- It must above all, be practical to appeal to the strong Pragmatic preferences.

- It must be soundly based and robust enough to survive the perfectionist scrutiny of the Theorists at middle and junior levels.

- It must be sufficiently novel and exciting to retain the enthusiastic involvement of the Activists at senior levels.

The idea of setting up a conventional series of off-the-job management training courses was rejected on the grounds that it would not appeal strongly enough to the Pragmatists nor would it be novel enough to win commitment from the Activists at the top. Instead, a formula that combined training and development with problem solving project work was arrived at by setting up a whole series of project groups to work on real issues under the guidance of a number of external trainers. This was seen to meet the needs identified by the questionnaire by being:-

- practical enough for Pragmatists

- soundly based for Theorists

- novel for Activists

- paced to suit the needs of the Reflectors (with four week gaps between sessions).

2. Identifying the preferences of course members before they attend a training course

The questionnaire can easily be incorporated into the nomination procedures before people attend in-company training programmes of various kinds. The questionnaire is sent out with any accompanying letter to prospective course members and returned to the training department for scoring and interpretation. Once the learning styles have been established a number of possibilities offer themselves. At the very least, advance warning about the predominant styles of the people coming together on a given course is useful for the trainer. It helps him/her prepare for the course and possibly slant parts of the programme to accommodate better the learning style preferences of the group. (See our article 'Developing the Skills for Matrix Management' as an example.) If there are a number of interchangeable trainers available to run a given programme then the trainer's style can be taken into account to get the most compatible match between learners and trainer.

A rather more ambitious possibility is to use the questionnaire information to allocate certain people to certain courses. For example, if it was felt desirable to have together on one course an equal number of Activists, Reflectors, Theorists and Pragmatists, this can be engineered by administering some sort of quota system. This ensures that the group, as a whole, is well balanced with all the different learning styles equally represented. If, on the other hand, it is considered more practical to have as homogeneous a group as possible then it is possible to invite say, Activists/Pragmatists to attend one course together and Reflectors/ Theorists to attend on a different occasion. The courses, whilst attempting to achieve the same objectives, are easier to plan and run with the likes and dislikes/strengths and weaknesses of more homogeneous target populations clearly in mind. The syllabus therefore remains the same but the methods differ to cater for learning style preferences. Thus, there could, for example, be lots of projects for Activists, reading time built in for Reflectors, question and answer sessions for Theorists and practical demonstrations for Pragmatists.

If it is considered impractical to offer different versions of the same course, then it might be considered more feasible to design different options or branches within the same programme. The course could contain some core activities standard for all irrespective of differences in learning style preferences. At intervals, however, the programme would split into branching activities tailor-made to meet the needs of people with specific learning styles.

Using learning styles during a training programme

This section contains several suggestions on how learning styles can be used to advantage during a training programme. The ideas are introduced in order of complexity starting with the simplest and progressing to the more substantial. The simple ideas are easy to 'graft on' to an existing training course; the more complex ideas usually involve more fundamental design work.

1.   Predicting learning difficulties

If the questionnaire is administered and scored at the start of a training programme the trainer can anticipate how course members are likely to behave during the course. For example, the questionnaire results help to anticipate who will:-

–   talk most and talk least

–   ask questions and whether the questions will probe basic assumptions or explore applications

–   find the course too fast/too slow

–   volunteer to 'take the chair' or present in plenary sessions

–   read handouts in the evenings or skimp them and prop up the bar instead

–   produce lots of off-the-top-of-the-head ideas or only produce prepared ones

- experiment with different ways of behaving or stick cautiously to the tried and true

- be keen to observe or be keen to take part

- be interested in feedback or want to move on without feedback

- be the first to call the office or be detached from what's going on 'back on the ranch'.

Predictions like these are useful because they open up the possibility of trainers being able to handle people more appropriately from the word go, rather than feeling their way for a period as behavioural tendencies gradually reveal themselves. So, for example, the questionnaire can help trainers 'identify' which people need explicitly bringing-in to the proceedings and how best to answer questions to the satisfaction of the questioner. All this helps trainers establish credibility with course members faster than might otherwise have been possible as well as helping them learn more effectively.

The questionnaire has been used to identify specific learning difficulties in advance of their occurrence. For example, the questionnaire has been found to be an accurate predictor of the sorts of inhibitions people will experience during a 'creative thinking' course. Briefly, Reflectors are likely to find the sheer pace at which creative thinking techniques generate ideas a major problem. Theorists are inhibited by their liking for logical thinking and dislike of untidy loose ends. Pragmatists with their dedication to things practical suffer from difficulties in suspending judgement during the generation of ideas. Activists have fewest problems with creative thinking but become impatient with the subsequent evaluation of the ideas generated.

Predictions of learning difficulties such as these are valuable because they help to indicate what the trainer can do to alleviate or avoid the difficulties. If the difficulties are the inevitable sort that simply have to be worked through as an essential part of the learning process, then at least the questionnaire helps the trainer to hold fast through the troughs and encourage learners to do the same.

The questionnaire results help to alert the participants to the parts of the learning cycle they are likely to find easy/enjoyable and difficult/irksome. Activists, for example, can be forewarned about the parts of the course that better suit Reflectors and Theorists. This helps them understand **why** they are temperamentally unsuited to, say, learning reviews and sets them the challenge of raising their tolerance for such things. Similarly Reflectors can be helped to realise why they prefer to shun the limelight and leave others to volunteer and go at risk.

The session described in chapter 2 is an admirable way of introducing learning, making the learning cycle explicit and showing the relevance and usefulness of questionnaire data.

2. Using questionnaire results to constitute groups, teams, or syndicates

Much has been written about methodologies for putting together individuals who can blend their different strengths to form a coherent team. The questionnaire offers another basis for mixing groups in a training situation. Perhaps the most obvious way to use learning styles as a basis for putting groups on courses together, is to ensure that all groups are matched and that the full range of learning styles are available to each group. Suppose, for example, there were 12 people together on a course and they were to be split into two syndicates with six members in each. The questionnaire scores for the total course are as follows:-

	A	R	T	P
Mike	6	(19)	(16)	12
Cathie	6	(16)	(15)	10
John	(12)	7	8	(17)
Peter	(13)	12	10	5
David	9	12	12	13
Bill	(14)	11	8	10
Sheila	(18)	10	8	13
Ian	10	(17)	(16)	(18)
Anita	9	7	(15)	(17)
Malcolm	(15)	6	7	7
Ruth	(16)	8	6	(16)
George	7	(17)	(15)	(18)

Circles indicate a strong style preference when the general norms on page 10 are applied to these scores.

Given these scores, the best way to match two syndicates would be as follows:-

Syndicate 1
Sheila	(A)
Peter	(A)
John	(A/P)
Ian	(R/T/P)
Mike	(R/T)
Anita	(T/P)

Syndicate 2
Bill	(A)
Malcolm	(A)
Ruth	(A/P)
George	(R/T/P)
Cathie	(R/T)
David	(average all rounder with no strong preferences).

We have conducted experiments where the performance of syndicates constituted at random have been compared with the performance of syndicates constituted on the basis of learning styles. The performance of syndicates with a full range of learning styles available to it has always been found to be superior. They are better at achieving set objectives, produce higher quality of work, meet deadlines more comfortably and interact more efficiently with less interrupting, more listening, more building, etc, etc. Success is still further enhanced if the learning styles of each syndicate member are made public. This seems to help syndicates to identify the relative strengths and weaknesses of its members and allocate roles in such a way that strengths are fully exploited.

Of course there may be good reasons for deliberately constituting groups on an entirely different basis. For example, it may be desirable to put all the Activists/Pragmatists together in one syndicate and all the Reflectors/Theorists together in another. This is a mixing technique which helps to create conditions where characteristically high contributors are somewhat curtailed and where low contributors have a chance to flower in an environment where their more dominant colleagues have been removed. Groups wholly of one style are unlikely to provide balanced learning experiences. Think of six Theorists together or six Activists!

3. Making the learning cycle explicit at intervals throughout the course

It helps to reinforce the learning process if at sensible intervals through the course the learning cycle is referred to. There are many opportunities to do this in the normal course of events. For example:-

–   When briefing participants for an exercise you can point out that the exercise itself is an experience.

–   When debriefing participants after an exercise you can ask them how the activity maps on to the reviewing and concluding stages in the cycle.

–   When introducing action planning activities you can link it to the concluding and planning stages in the cycle.

It is a good idea to have the learning cycle on permanent display throughout the course and use it often to provide 'you are here' pointers.

4. Building in pauses and learning reviews

Many trainers feel compelled (perhaps because they have Activist preferences) to keep the pressure on throughout a training programme. There is a feeling that unless participants are busy doing something each waking moment then they are not learning. This is the equivalent of activity traps at work where people rush around keeping busy for the sake of keeping busy. The learning cycle helps us to appreciate that experiencing is only part of what is involved in learning. Scheduling time for reviewing, concluding and planning is crucial to get the balance right. Nor is it good enough to have reviewing as an optional overnight activity. It needs to be scheduled in prime time between each experience.

Pauses for reflection are made more purposeful if participants are encouraged to use a structured approach. Written learning logs are one way of doing this. Group learning reviews, where participants draw up lists of lessons learned, agree some conclusions and consequential plans, are another way. Of course, Reflectors may like this process more than others. It can be helpful to set up pair reviews, with contrasting styles.

Whatever the details of the method, the essential point is that learning reviews need to be unashamedly incorporated into the structure of the course. This sends out messages about taking learning seriously and the importance of giving equal weight to all stages in the learning cycle.

5. Getting people to expand their repertoire of learning styles

If you assume that in a perfect world everyone would have balanced learning style preferences, thus equipping them to do all stages in the learning cycle with consummate ease, it helps to encourage people deliberately to practise using underdeveloped styles.

The best way to do this is to get each participant to focus on the style with the lowest score and write out a list of the relevant questionnaire items that they crossed. This procedure is described fully in the booklet 'Using Your Learning Styles' so we will not give all the details here. The key to success in setting people the challenge of developing a style which is not already a characteristic one for them is undoubtedly to encourage them to set realistic, yet specific, personal action plans. We suggest usually working on only one or two items at a time.

People who want to develop the Activist style could, for example, set themselves a specific target to contribute a minimum amount at each discussion session ("*I will speak for at least two unbroken minutes for every thirty minutes worth of plenary session*"). People who want to develop their Reflector style could plan to volunteer to act as observers at least once per day and set themselves targets for their diligence as observers ("*I will write down verbatim at least 50% of what people say*"). People who want to develop their Theorist style could plan to search for the basic assumptions underpinning the various subjects being studied on the course ("*I will identify and list at least five assumptions for each topic introduced on the course and verify them with the presenter*"). Finally, people who want to develop their Pragmatist tendencies could plan to identify practical techniques for each subject encountered on the course ("*I will identify and list at least two techniques for each course topic, describing them in 'how to do it' terms such that anyone on the course could action them correctly*").

These are, of course, only examples. There are many possible action plans that could result from a careful analysis of the questionnaire items. Whatever plans emerge, it is useful to list them on flip charts and leave them on permanent display. This helps to act as a reminder and aids collaboration and mutual support between course members as they struggle to develop uncharacteristic behaviour patterns. If need be, time to review progress with personal action plans arising from learning styles and produce updated plans could be scheduled at the start of each day.

6. Using questionnaire results to allocate roles in exercises

Often, within the framework of an exercise on a course, trainers are able to decide which roles to distribute to which participants. Role playing exercises are an obvious opportunity to do this but other exercises may also lend themselves. For example, it may be appropriate to designate a leader or chairperson for a team work exercise or syndicate activity. Learning style preferences can be a useful way to allocate such roles and this can be done in two different ways. When the objective is to give people roles that they are capable of carrying off convincingly, then the roles should be allocated so that they are compatible with learning style strengths. Alternatively, when the objective is to encourage people to develop behaviours that are not already comfortably within their repertoire, the trainer can allocate roles that challenge people to overcome their learning style weaknesses.

An example is an exercise at the start of an interactive skills course, where course members who get high Reflector/Theorist questionnaire scores are put together in a group. They are given the following task to tackle: 'Prepare to interview the trainer for 30 minutes to find out everything you need to know about this course'. Meanwhile, high scoring Activists and Pragmatists are given some guidelines on how to observe, and time to prepare to do a detailed observation of the interview. All this is done quite openly with the full knowledge of everyone involved. In fact, it is important that the rationale for allocating roles is public knowledge so that people do not waste energy being suspicious of the trainer's motives.

Another example of using questionnaire results as the basis for allocating roles is an exercise which has been used to help people practice the skills involved in participating in effective meetings. Six different roles are distributed in the form of objectives that each person is requested to achieve by the end of the meeting. In summary the roles are as follows:-

- **Objective 1**
  To have got your colleagues to agree a formal objective for the meeting and to have used it to review the success of the meeting.

- **Objective 2**
  To have 'chaired' the discussion effectively.

- **Objective 3**
  To have been an effective contributor of ideas.

- **Objective 4**
  To have been an effective 'devil's advocate'.

- **Objective 5**
  To have been an effective 'catalyst'.

- **Objective 6**
  To have been an effective developer of other people's ideas.

There are no hard and fast rules for the allocation of these roles, but more often than not they are distributed in a way that challenges each participant to go out on a limb and experiment with ways of behaving that do not come 'naturally'. In this case the objectives are allocated on the following basis:-

- **Objective 1**
  To an Activist

- **Objective 2**
  To a Reflector or Activist

- **Objective 3**
  To a Reflector

- **Objective 4**
  To a Pragmatist or Activist

- **Objective 5**
  To a Theorist

- **Objective 6**
  To a Theorist or Pragmatist.

Using learning styles after a training programme

We conclude this chapter by giving ideas to the trainer on how to use the questionnaire by looking at the implications of learning styles for follow-up activities.

1. Producing plans to implement what has been learned

Most courses conclude with some 'bridge building' to help people survive the perils of transferring what has been learned on the course to the very different circumstances of the on-the-job situation. This involves action planning where participants are invited to take stock of what they have learned, the working situation to which they are about to return (warts and all), and the likely hazards in continuing to develop new found skills or apply new knowledge. Obviously a person's learning style preferences should be taken into account in reaching feasible action plans. Also we suggest that the learning style of the person's boss should loom large in any end-of- course planning. Particularly pertinent here is the list on pages 56-59 of the different types of support likely to emerge from bosses with different learning styles. They can be reproduced as useful handouts for course members to refer to as they produce their action plans.

If course members are paired off to help each other produce action plans then Pragmatists are invaluable and should never be paired together. It is much more useful to spread people with Pragmatist tendencies around so that they can use their skills to help tether Activists, Reflectors and Theorists to reality when it comes to producing action plans that are really feasible. Pairing different strong preferences is also very productive.

2. Getting course members to check the learning styles of bosses, subordinates and colleagues

Provided course members have been shown the ropes adequately when it comes to administering the questionnaire, scoring it, and applying appropriate norms to the results, we see no objection to encouraging them to give the questionnaire to people who are likely to have an impact on their day-to-day learning. Bosses are obviously key figures in this regard but subordinates and colleagues are also likely candidates. If course members are reticent about administering the questionnaire themselves, without any 'expert' help, then the trainer can offer to come and do it as part of the 'after-sales-service' following a training course of some kind. Besides being helpful in its own right, such a questionnaire session with a real work team can act as an effective *entrée* for the trainer - especially if he/she is adept at interpreting the questionnaire and counselling interested parties in its implications.

3. Running follow-up workshops

Questionnaire results should always be kept for future reference and are especially useful if it is planned to hold follow-up workshops at some interval after the initial training. An example is the offer of a one day workshop, on an entirely voluntary basis, four to eight months after attendance on the initial training programme. Where numbers and administrative arrangements permit, it has been found that the workshop is enhanced if Activists, Reflectors, Theorists and Pragmatists attend in more or less equal numbers. This is because the learning styles have a significant effect on the problems of application people are likely to have encountered in the period since they attended the course. Any review of the successes people have notched up, and the difficulties they have encountered, is enriched by having a broad spectrum of learning styles present. To some extent they counter-balance one another in a way that can be mutually supportive and stimulate fresh efforts to overcome transfer problems.

Follow-ups are also a golden opportunity to re-administer the questionnaire to see if there have been any significant changes as a result of the training and subsequent back at work experiences. If the training had been aimed at helping people to become all-round learners, it is clearly important to see if the questionnaire retest results confirm this tendency. In these circumstances the questionnaire acts as one means of validating the success of the training in achieving this objective.

Conclusion

We hope this chapter has provided plenty of thought starters on how information on learning style preferences can be used before, during and after off-the-job programmes. Since learning is supposed to be the name of the game on all such programmes, it is bordering on the criminal not to make the process explicit and in so doing help people to learn more effectively than they otherwise would.

CHAPTER 5

HELPING TO CREATE PERSONAL DEVELOPMENT PLANS

A personal development plan is a tailor made statement of needs for enhanced performance, with suggested activities to meet those needs. The major contribution of learning styles to such plans is the assistance given to the selection of learning opportunities that are congruent with the preferences of the learner. Will a low Theorist learn from a lecture full of concepts and models?

The design of a personal development plan can follow two learning styles strategies. One is to suggest activities which match strong styles and avoid low styles, choosing activities congruent with existing styles. This avoids the likelihood of people being exposed to learning experiences in a form which they find unhelpful. It reduces frustration, though it does not maximise the opportunities or the learning.

A second strategy is to build a wider range of learning effectiveness by deliberately providing activities not congruent with preferences. In our view this is the preferred strategy but only if the trainer can provide explanation, encouragement and support, probably through a Learning to Learn workshop. Without this support, the selection of activities with which the learner is likely to have difficulty is inefficient, irresponsible, or both.

This strategy is therefore likely to involve a personal development plan through which a learner develops his or her less preferred styles. It is also likely that many people will be less enthusiastic about doing this simply 'to become a better learner' but will do it in order 'to be able to learn from activity X something important to my effectiveness'.

The improvement of an individual's capacity to learn from a variety of activities by building additional learning strengths is covered explicitly in the booklet 'Using Your Learning Styles', and the detail is not repeated here. The fact that a learner has a strong preference for a style does not mean that he or she necessarily actually uses the style to full effect.

It is important to emphasise when discussing styles that no single style has an overwhelming advantage over any other. Each has strengths and weaknesses, but the strengths may be especially important in one situation, whilst not in another.

We see the relative strengths and weaknesses of each learning style as follows:-

Activists
Strengths:
- Flexible and open-minded.
- Happy to have a go.
- Happy to be exposed to new situations.
- Optimistic about anything new and therefore unlikely to resist change.

Weaknesses:
- Tendency to take the immediately obvious action without thinking.
- Often take unnecessary risks.
- Tendency to do too much themselves and hog the limelight.
- Rush into action without sufficient preparation.
- Get bored with implementation/consolidation.

Reflectors
Strengths:
- Careful.
- Thorough and methodical.
- Thoughtful.
- Good at listening to others and assimilating information.
- Rarely jump to conclusions.

Weaknesses:
- Tendency to hold back from direct participation.
- Slow to make up their minds and reach a decision.
- Tendency to be too cautious and not take enough risks.
- Not assertive - they aren't particularly forthcoming and have no 'small talk'.

Theorists
Strengths:
- Logical 'vertical' thinkers.
- Rational and objective.
- Good at asking probing questions.
- Disciplined approach.

Weaknesses:
- Restricted in lateral thinking.
- Low tolerance for uncertainty, disorder and ambiguity.
- Intolerant of anything subjective or intuitive.
- Full of 'shoulds, oughts and musts'.

Pragmatists
Strengths:
- Keen to test things in practice.
- Practical, down to earth, realistic.
- Businesslike - get straight to the point.
- Technique oriented.

Weaknesses:
- Tendency to reject anything without an obvious application.
- Not very interested in theory or basic principles.

- Tendency to seize on the first expedient solution to a problem.
- Impatient with what they see as waffle.
- On balance, task oriented not people oriented.

These general statements about how individuals respond to work situations must be associated with the more specific statements about responses to learning situations, spelled out in chapter 3.

Initiation of personal development plans

These plans may be created in a variety of circumstances:

Courses

Many courses nowadays include one or more sessions towards the end on personal action plans. This basically good idea is often spoiled by over optimism, by unrealistic assessment of the circumstances to which the learner is returning, by failure to use the principles of the learning cycle and learning styles.

Where action plans arise from a Learning to Learn session (see chapter 7), from a workshop on self or personal development, or a development centre, these problems are less likely to be ignored - but specific discussion on individual styles must be designed in.

Learning reviews and learning logs are now frequently suggested or used on courses. Trainers ought not to be surprised that Activists often reject them, while Reflectors respond enthusiastically. If the trainer has time to work on this problem, then strategy 2 mentioned above comes into play. For example the trainer might ask *"what kind of note do you keep now about important decisions or events. How could you build on that?"*

Development centres/self development workshops

It is in our view especially ironic, to be polite, that anyone should design a centre or workshop with development as its explicit focus without using the cycle or styles - unless they have some other process which provides equivalent depth. The cycle and individual learning preferences are fundamental. For examples see the bibliography especially Honey and Povah, and Butler.

Appraisal (or performance review)

Recommendations for further training and development are often part of appraisal. They can be better matched to individual styles, as illustrated throughout this Manual.

Counselling

Counselling may involve help on some personal or managerial style problem. Alternatively counselling can be directed at much larger longer term issues such as future career moves or remedies for personal problems. In either case 'learning' solutions will be more effective if related to the learning cycle and learning styles.

Personal development discussions

Some organisations separate issues of development from those of performance review. Again suggestions about the kind of actions which need to be taken will be more effective when learning preferences are considered.

Learning agreements

The idea of learning agreements between an organisation and its employees has been encouraged in the UK by among others the Management Charter Initiative and the Association for Management Education and Development. If learning preferences were taken into account, such agreements would be more effective.

Learning contracts

These differ from agreements not only in the apparent legality conveyed by the word, but also by the fact that contract is the term used in education or training institutions as a formal process of negotiation between trainer and learner. Originally the contract, although concerned with content and process, rarely took account of learning styles. Now a few institutions recognise the need. Read 'Using Learning Contracts' by Malcolm Knowles, Jossey Bass, 1986 for the principles, and George Boak for the association of learning styles and learning contracts (see bibliography).

In helping to devise a personal development plan we suggest therefore that the trainer keeps the cycle and learning styles in mind, after identifying the development need.

As an example, we take the familiar case in which it is suggested that a manager's skills in running a meeting need to be improved. Should the trainer recommend, for example, a book, a course, observation, coaching? All of these? We recommend the trainer to consider amongst other things:-

- What is the learning style of the individual?

- If considering a course, what style if any does it favour? Does it provide appropriate emphasis on all stages of the cycle? (Many skills courses give insufficient time to Reflecting and Concluding.)

- If observing a skilled performer is to be recommended, is the individual a strong Reflector who will need little help to use the opportunity, or a strong Theorist who may be unhappy with the absence of guiding principles?

- If coaching is a possibility, how well matched are the styles of coach and learner? (See the next chapter for more detail on this.)

- Other examples of selecting activities in relation to styles are given in chapter 3.

Self development

Self development can, of course, be stimulated through any of the processes indicated above, even though the initiative and perhaps the early stimulus comes from the organisation as expressed through a manager's manager or adviser.

However, it is also true that a great deal of development occurs at the initiative of the individual with no or very little organisational input. While the fact of the extent to which managers and professional people learn most of what they do learn on and through the job has always been known, only in recent years has work started to be done on improving the consciousness and effectiveness of 'natural' 'real time' learning from experience. It has been one of our own interests to contribute to this (see especially 'The Manual of Learning Opportunities' and 'The Opportunist Learner'). However self development processes can share with any other kind of learning process the weakness of failing to relate learning preferences to the proposed activity and we have commented on that weakness (see 'Self Development: Missing Elements' in bibliography).

Your personal choice

We hope trainers, as people wishing to advise others on learning, have personal development plans. It may be entirely the trainer's own idea or one which has been developed through institutional or organisational initiative.

Here is a personal exercise for trainers, who may wish to tackle it without help, or by looking at 'Using Your Learning Styles'.

Stage 1

Take one of the issues on which you want to develop yourself. Look at your own learning style preference or antipathy, if any, and try and decide what kind of activity would best suit your learning style preference in tackling that issue.

Stage 2

Then as a further development, try and think of ways of dealing with the issue which would suit each of the four learning style preferences.

Stage 3

Finally, think about how this exercise relates to the cycle and learning styles.

Final comment

We have added this exercise as an illustration of the planning stage of the cycle. We expect it to be particularly attractive to the Pragmatists and to the Activist who may be dying to 'do something' at this point in the Manual. Of course, Reflectors will enjoy 'thinking about my needs'. The Theorist will like the intellectual challenge of stage 2. Further discussion on the trainer as learner will be found in chapter 8.

CHAPTER 6

PEOPLE WHO HELP DEVELOPMENT

Trainers are, or ought to be, professionals in helping others to learn. Some of their work will be directly with individual managers or groups of managers, working on their own learning plans, their own learning preferences and their own learning processes. In addition however trainers may want to help managers help those who report to them. This chapter shows how this may be done.

Alan Mumford's book 'Management Development: Strategies for Action' has a chapter on this subject and is important reading in order to put this chapter into a wider context.

The people who may help the development of others, and who therefore need to know and understand the learning cycle and learning styles are :-

- Bosses
- Grandbosses
- Mentors
- Clients for projects/task groups etc.
- Colleagues
- Subordinates

In addition, managers may be helped by friends outside work, and by a domestic partner.

How to interest managers in learning style preferences

One way of generating interest in managers is through their participation on a Learning to Learn session as illustrated in the next chapter.

Another way is to create the opportunity for one to one discussion between trainer and manager, perhaps from a question such as *"shall we send X on a course on interpersonal skills?"* The trainer can, after clarifying needs, move into *"what is he likely to respond to best as a learner?"*

The influence of the manager's own learning preferences

One of the results of either of the processes suggested above is that managers are made aware of the fact that they may have strong learning preferences themselves, and that they are likely to choose for others activities which would suit them but, do not necessarily suit those others.

Since no learning style is 'better' than any other, a more effective learning environment can be created if people use differences positively. On the other hand, where people are unaware, or make no attempt to use differences positively, then differences can be very unhelpful. For example, a strongly Reflector boss with an equally strongly Activist subordinate will initially create a very unhelpful learning relationship.

The same general principle is true with colleagues, where differences can be helpful in creating a diversity of learning input, or can be unhelpful because people get annoyed by the differences.

How the boss can use learning styles

The trainer may have to equip the boss with the knowledge necessary to stimulate him to use learning styles. An example is a manager who attends a major management course at the direct cost of £10,000. The trainer may be able to show that the course has been particularly useful because it fitted the manager's learning style, or it might have been an unfortunate experience because it favoured a different style (see chapter 3 for examples where this might apply). Similarly, a boss who has been encouraged to look at management activities as providing learning opportunities may also need to be reminded that the way in which an individual learns will influence the actual utility of the opportunity. To ask someone to observe a negotiation with a supplier when the individual has a low Reflector score is unlikely to be a productive suggestion (unless some other action is also taken).

In the best of all worlds bosses will be dealing with individuals who have a high range of potential to learn because they have high scores in all styles. More often, however, people will have a mixture of strong and low preferences and decisions need to be made about the relevance of particular kinds of opportunity. For the moment we will concentrate on suggestions about how a boss should use questionnaire results to identify opportunities which are congruent with any learning style preference a subordinate may have. We have two reasons for suggesting this as the first strategy:-

–   There are not many bosses who will give a serious amount of time to any kind of development discussion.

–   Even those who give time, may not get very far if they have to identify not only opportunities but also how to help someone whose learning style is not congruent with them.

The strategy of trying to build learning strengths, although one which we value, requires time and attention rather than simply a direction 'you had better try and improve your Reflector style'.

Of course willingness to invest time may itself be an indication of the preferred learning style of the boss. It is predictable that highly Activist bosses will be less likely to give time than if they were strongly Reflector or Theorist. It may be hoped therefore that the trainer and the boss will have clarified the desirable objective, which may be a mixture of what the boss is prepared to attempt and what the subordinate might really benefit from. After this the appropriate steps are:-

1. The boss reviews the questionnaire results with subordinates, and discusses how valid they are. In our experience disagreements about validity are extremely rare. If there is disagreement about the preferences indicated by the subordinate's results, the boss could be asked to do a questionnaire on the subordinate.

2. The boss should review his own learning style and compare with his subordinate. (The implication obviously is that the boss will have done the questionnaire himself - at least he should be asked to produce a good estimate based on the general descriptions. But it is much preferable that he does the questionnaire.) This comparison will lead to the possibility of the boss identifying some things which he is likely to be able to provide himself because he sees them as natural, and others which he is less likely to see as appropriate for the individual. A strongly Reflector boss for example might well suggest activities congruent with that style, and might respond to the idea that he and the subordinate should get together from time to time to discuss learning experiences. An Activist boss is likely to throw opportunities at a subordinate, but give little time to discuss them.

3. The boss should review the kind of learning opportunities which can be provided. A checklist such as the following could be used for this.

Formal Learning Opportunities	**Informal Learning Opportunities**
Being coached	Job change within same function
Being counselled	Job change to a new function
Having a mentor	Same job with additional responsibilities
Job rotation	Boss
Secondments	Mentor
Stretched boundaries	Colleagues / Peers
Special projects	Subordinates
Committees	Network contacts
Task groups	Projects
External activities	Familiar tasks
Internal courses	Unfamiliar tasks
External courses	Task groups
Reading	Problem solving with colleagues
	Domestic life
	Voluntary work
	Professional groups
	Social committees
	Sporting clubs

Here again the boss might choose to learn from such opportunities in one way, but the subordinate in another. The issue will be whether the boss wants to propose that someone with a strong learning style takes advantage of that, or whether it is suggested that the subordinate attempts to build additional strengths.

The main thing that bosses can do is identify and use different learning opportunities within their own domain. They may have, for example, the authority to decide that subordinates accompany them on visits to important customers. Outside their own domain managers may need to persuade others to provide help. They might want to offer subordinates as secretaries to task groups or committees, or recommend them for particular courses, or suggest that they are involved in projects, or want to use someone else to recommend 'the best book on the subject'.

Here are two examples of a manager using learning styles to help someone else make a decision about a learning opportunity.

Case A

A manager has received details of two seminars on employee involvement. One seminar emphasises the quality of speakers including well known names from the European Commission and sessions such as 'concepts and models of employee involvement'. The other seminar emphasises that a number of practical exercises will be provided demonstrating the issues which will arise.

Since the subordinate will be involved in introducing a new process of employee involvement, it is agreed he could benefit from some formal training. Questionnaire results show him as a strong Pragmatist and low Theorist. They review the alternative together and agree that the latter seminar fits the learning style best. (Other issues about the choice are omitted here.)

Case B

A manager has a senior assistant who attends a number of important meetings with her. It is the manager's style to ask her subordinates for comments about the meeting. The subordinate is careful, analytical and relatively low profile at meetings, not given to taking risks. He has a strong Reflector and a low Activist score. They agree that one consequence of the subordinate's style is that he may have too low a visibility from the point of view of other people's perception of his current contribution and potential for other jobs. They agree together that instead of encouraging him to take a more active role, he will seek and his boss will offer feedback on the nature and effectiveness of the contributions he actually makes. This is a strategy of building from an existing strength rather than trying to transform his style into a 'have a go' approach.

The contributions of different styles of bosses

Where a boss has a choice of the kind indicated in the previous two cases, it is quite likely that whatever his or her style he or she could be encouraged to take an organised rational view. However most learning depends on relatively immediate reactions to on the job situations. Here, the preferences of the boss will take a more natural and therefore in some cases less structured and analytical form. For example, Activist bosses will provide experiences as an immediate response to situations and will happily throw subordinates in 'at the deep end'. Such bosses will not provide systematic, analytic experiences. Equally, strong Reflector bosses will want to organise the learning experience in advance and expect a serious review after the event. They will be less likely to encourage subordinates to take chances and risks.

Our views about the ways in which different styles would influence what a boss may offer are:-

The Activist boss

Activists tend to help by:-

- Generating (unconsciously) opportunities for others to observe and reflect on what they do.

- Taking an optimistic and positive view of what is involved in a new situation.

- Giving a positive and encouraging lead, at least initially, in short term active learning activities.

- Following through with action to provide learning experiences **if** they have been convinced of their value.

- Responding spontaneously to opportunities as they arise.

Activists will be less likely to provide help through:-

- Providing planned learning experiences.

- Giving support to learning as a planned, structured activity.

- Assessing and using learning experiences which are different from those through which they learned.

- Discussing learning opportunities beforehand and reviewing them afterwards.

- Standing back and allowing others to participate or take action.

- Giving a good personal model of planned learner behaviour.

- Giving different learning experiences to subordinates with different learning styles.

The Reflector boss

Reflectors will tend to help by:-

- Suggesting activities which can be observed.

- Recommending how observation can be carried out.

- Identifying ways in which an event or a problem can be analysed.

- Discussing what may happen, and reviewing what has happened.

- Providing data or feedback in a controlled learning situation.

- Advising on how to prepare carefully for a management activity.

- Not taking a dominant role in meetings with subordinates.

- Emphasising the importance of collecting data before acting.

- Giving a considered response to requests for help.

Reflectors will be less likely to provide help through:-

- Suggesting ad hoc immediate learning opportunities.

- Showing how to take advantage spontaneously of unplanned learning activities.

- Providing unexpected or slightly risky learning situations, eg a sudden delegation of a task.

- Giving immediate answers to unexpected requests for direct help.

- Providing a large scale view of philosophy, concept, system or policy.

- Providing a strong personal model of anything except Reflector behaviour.

The Theorist boss

Theorists will tend to help by:-

- Showing interest in any intellectually respectable idea.

- Helping people to describe underlying causes, to explain the systems or concepts involved in an activity.

- Demonstrating the intellectual validity of an answer or process.

- Showing how to strengthen or demolish a case by the use of logic.

- Bringing out complexities.

- Aiming for clarity of structure of purpose.

- Articulating theories, eg Open Systems Theory or Total Quality Management.

- Generalising reasons why something works or does not work.

- Setting high standards in the quality of data.

Theorists will be less likely to provide help through:-

- Showing when to accept the obvious.

- Helping others to understand emotions and feelings in specific circumstances.

- Making use of data or occasions which conflict with their theories.

- Developing others who are different in intellectual quality or style, eg if perceived as lower calibre, or if theories clash with their own.

- Showing how to use information which **they** regard as trivial, irrelevant or intellectually not respectable.

- Drawing up specific action plans.

The Pragmatist boss

Pragmatists will tend to help by:-

- Showing responsiveness to new ideas and techniques.

- Demonstrating interest in specific action plans.

- Pressing for relevant learning programmes with clear pay off.

- Being open to new situations.

- Showing a belief in the possibility of improvement.

- Following the party line on, eg appraisals or releasing people for courses.

- Following specific suggestions on how to improve learning.

Pragmatists will be less likely to provide help through:-

- Being responsive to ideas or techniques not immediately relevant to a current problem.

- Showing interest in concepts or theories.

- Encouraging action relevant to the longer term.

- Encouraging ideas or learning programmes that they regard as unproven or way out.

- Pushing for action which is apparently not valued by the culture or system.

- Using learning opportunities which they see as divorced from real life, eg secondments outside the organisation, sessions by 'people who don't know our kind of industry/organisation/ problem'.

Clearly, if bosses know what kind of learning activities they are unlikely to provide they may be (and of course in terms of managerial responsibility, ought to be) at least responsive to suggestions outside their own style. The best bosses will indeed positively seek to fill in the gaps by using other people and resources.

How other helpers can use learning styles

Although their relationship with the learner will be different, the same principles apply to mentors, learning project clients, colleagues and subordinates.

How well does their style match with that of the person they are trying to help to learn?

How well do any proposals they have for suggested learning activities match the preferred learning style of the learner?

Mentors may be used very deliberately to provide a learning style different from that of an individual's boss. The learning style relationship between mentor and *protégé* has not been discussed in the literature, but the absence of 'fit' can be a major cause of an unsuccessful relationship.

Colleagues, learning groups and the learning organisation

Some of the grander pronouncements about the learning organisation ignore the fact that the organisation consists of individual learners. We have provided through the Learning Diagnostic Questionnaire, in 'The Manual of Learning Opportunities', one way of diagnosing the extent to which an organisation is supportive or otherwise of learning. Any personal development plan must recognise the realities of the kind of opportunities that are provided and those which will not be provided within that organisation.

Whatever the general nature of the organisation, managers will get more or less support from particular bosses or colleagues within it. We think that the creation of groups of people who try and help each other to learn will be another major step in the potential for productivity in learning within organisations. Most of us as trainers are very familiar with this in the course context. We deliberately create groups of people who we hope will help each other to learn. We may do it through relatively traditional processes of syndicates or subgroups, or less traditional processes such as Action Learning. Ideas on the effective creation of learning groups within courses have already been discussed in chapter 4.

Here we want to emphasise the possibility for an individual manager, working to some kind of personal development plan, to use the support and help of colleagues in the business (or even occasionally outside it). In addition to the individual and particular contacts which we have indicated earlier under 'helpers' - individual colleagues at work or friends outside - it is possible to create or facilitate the creation of groups of managers who will work on issues or problems together. Such groups will be more effective if they share together their learning style preferences - and if they are mixed in their strong preferences. A course or workshop may stimulate this kind of thing, where a group of managers decide to continue some kind of learning association after the course is over. Our experience is that people working in small groups, or perhaps even pairs, can be very helpful to each other in suggesting alternative ideas and alternative processes.

CHAPTER 7

DESIGNING LEARNING TO LEARN SESSIONS

In chapter 2 we gave an example of a 90 minute session to explain the learning cycle and learning styles. In this chapter we present more, and longer, sessions.

We believe in making the learning process explicit and open for discussion because it makes for more effective learning. Not only should trainers use the principles of the cycle and styles when designing programmes; they should also help participants to understand their own preferences. This increases the demand for relevant experiences on any programme. It is also the best way of trying to turn learning as a life long process from a *cliché* into improved reality. The process described here is also vital for enabling learners to take advantage of learning where it mainly occurs, namely on the job.

General principles of design

Of course, any Learning to Learn process should itself illustrate the issues it is raising. So the learning group should have an experience, review it and other experiences, draw conclusions and draw up action plans. Even a short 90 minute session can embrace all these.

As with any programme, the trainer may choose to enter the cycle at the stage most suitable to the situation and to the participants. So the session might start with a past learning experience, or with a task as a vehicle, or with a statement of the theory of adult learning.

It is very desirable to integrate this with other sessions on the programme by asking questions such as:

–   What parts of the learning cycle did we cover in working on 'interpersonal skills'?

–   Which learning styles were best suited by the session on finance?

Length

We have designed Learning to Learn sessions for a variety of different needs with different groups. The shortest has been a 90 minute session on one-day programmes on personal development, or effective management development. The middle position has been three to four hours on a longer programme for the development of directors. The longest period for managers (not in one complete day) has been on an MBA programme, where we devote about eight hours to this, within a two week start up process. We have run 2-day workshops for trainers, covering all the issues discussed in this Manual.

Materials

In addition to this Manual, trainers will need to have blank questionnaires, score sheets and general descriptions. Trainers may have their own transparencies. A copy of 'Using Your Learning Styles' for each participant should be provided.

Preparation

The first step is to give the questionnaire to participants. Wherever possible this is sent out in advance, because this gives the best opportunity to analyse the results for the group.

Trainers must compare their own questionnaire score with that of any group which is to receive the benefits of the Learning to Learn session. As a group trainers are higher on the Activist dimension than any other group of managers (except sales people!). Trainers should check whether their preferences affect the methods they use; are they right for this group?

The next step is to go through the list of individual scores, highlighting cases of strong or very strong preferences and low or very low preferences. This can be done either by using abbreviations vs/s/l/vl or by showing actual scores and ringing them in colours. This provides two different kinds of information. First it will tell you whether you have a widely distributed range and level of scores in the group as the following example shows.

Range of scores in a group

	Activist	Reflector	Theorist	Pragmatist
Highest Score	15	20	17	16
Lowest Score	4	5	7	9

Secondly, it will tell you whether you have a particularly strong or low preference amongst the majority. For example, in a group of 21 top executives 17 had a score of strong or very strong on the Theorist dimension.

The trainer will need to prepare either a transparency or flip chart illustrating the scores - if necessary without inserting the names of participants.

Timing

There are several options on where best to place Learning to Learn sessions. One possibility is to place the session right at the beginning of a workshop or programme, because it explains so much of what the participant will experience. Our preference is to build the session on the experience they will already have had during the programme, where at all possible. This means that often we do it in the afternoon of a one day programme, or on the third day of a ten day course. There are two reasons for this. One is that we always need to remember that the learning process however fascinating to us as trainers has usually a much lower priority amongst managers. We can confidently say that the majority actually like working on these issues - but most prefer to do so when they have been helped to see the relevance through some other activity. Of course if you were working with a group of Theorists, who are much more likely to be interested in information for its own sake providing it has a substantial conceptual base, then your strategy might be different!

From the trainer's point of view also, it is obviously helpful if you can refer to experiences on the course to illustrate the point - how people reacted to a brilliantly delivered lecture, the different ways in which people got value from a simulation or game.

Content

There are essentially three elements:-

–   The total learning process expressed through the learning cycle.

–   The definitions of learning styles.

–   How to select appropriate activities, or to build additional learning strengths.

Element 1 - The Learning Cycle

The trainer needs transparencies showing the learning cycle, the task cycle (see below) and the learning cycle with learning styles (see page 7) .

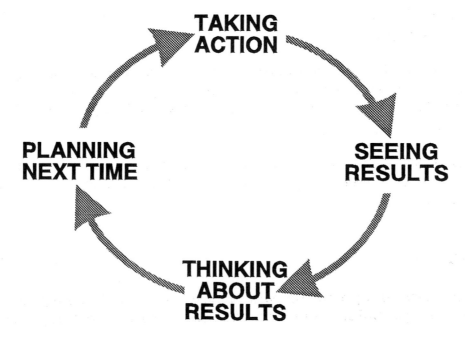

If time and the interests of the group allow, it is helpful to start with the task cycle. This helps to establish the commonality between the thinking processes that go into carrying out tasks, and the processes involved in learning. So a possible sequence is:-

- show the task cycle

- show the learning cycle

- show and discuss task and learning cycle.

The discussion of the learning cycle is itself an interesting representation of how to use learning styles in designing these sessions. If the group includes a significant number of high Theorists, then the cycle should be put up front and quite a bit of time spent on it. If the group is low on Theorists but high on Pragmatists, then the trainer may choose to show the learning cycle more briefly, and move on to the specific styles within this group.

Element 2 - Learning Styles

Option 1

Start with the transparency showing the learning cycle and learning styles, and make a statement such as:-

"If we were all equally effective at all stages of the cycle, we would have potential to be good learners from all kinds of activity. Unfortunately, people are not all equally effective at all stages and they may have preferences for one or more stage. Any preference can be identified through the Learning Styles Questionnaire, which you have done. Let us look first at what the words mean."

Then go over:-

-     The general descriptions (in full).

-     The will learn well from/will learn less well from lists in 'Using Your Learning Styles' (it is sensible to be selective on these, not covering every line).

The next step is to show a transparency on the general norms, or other norms you wish to use. The 'Using Your Learning Styles' booklet can also be referred to. Then the trainer can expose the result for this group (transparency or flip). It is always best at this point to check that people have understood the concept of norms. (See chapter 2.)

The next requirement is to establish validity. Depending on the size of the main group, and rooms available, the trainer can set up sub groups or pairs to undertake a task such as:-

-     How accurately do you think the questionnaire results describe your learning style preference?

–   What information do you have to support your view, from past learning experiences on this course and on other occasions?

–   What information do you have from other people (especially fellow course members) confirming or disconfirming your view?

–   What points do you want to take back for discussion in the full plenary session?

The trainer may be faced with questions from individuals or groups about issues of validity and reliability. See chapter 2 for common questions and answers on the questionnaire.

Option 2

Instead of moving straight into the display and discussion of questionnaire results, participants can be given the following exercise (which can be done in full group).

–   Review your two most helpful learning experiences. What were they and what made them helpful?

–   Review your two least helpful learning experiences. What were they and what made them unhelpful?

–   Identify at least one of each which you can discuss publicly.

The trainer can then capture answers on two flip charts - helpful and unhelpful.

As the next stage the trainer can draw out those factors about the reasons which relate to the cycle and learning styles. While it is possible to identify stages on the cycle with reasonable certainty from these comments, attribution of styles is more risky, so the following examples are illustrative not wholly certain. Likely comments will include:-

–   It was a completely theoretical presentation - no hints of how to apply it (low Theorist).

–   There was too much talking, not enough doing (strong Activist).

–   We rushed around with lots of exercises - no time to think (strong Reflector).

–   The exercises were absolutely spot on for my job (high Pragmatist).

–   My boss never had time to discuss what I had achieved through the project (strong Reflector).

–   I had a mentor who reviewed my work with me every week, and helped me sort out how the different aspects related (strong Theorist).

In addition to comments which help develop the idea of the learning cycle and learning styles, it is quite likely that the same kind of experience will appear from different people as helpful and unhelpful. For example, on one course we found outdoor training appearing on each chart.

The trainer can draw out from the flip charts the conclusions that:-

- People learn differently, well or badly, from the same kind of experience.

- People tend to avoid repeating previously unhelpful experiences. *"Never expect your boss to be helpful"; "I would never go on that kind of course again".*

At this stage the trainer can move into the approach spelled out in Option 1.

Element 3 - Improving Learning Styles

Once the validity of an individual's results have been established, participants can move into answering the question 'so what?' They can be shown the learning cycle and asked what stages have been covered so far. They should be able to identify that they:-

- have been through an experience (their experience on this session and a past learning experience)

- reflected on the experience, and on the data they have been given on learning styles

- drew conclusions about learning styles and themselves as learners.

With little prompting they will see that to complete the cycle they should 'plan the next steps'. In order to do this, they should be given 'Using Your Learning Styles'. We will not repeat the detailed suggestions here. As we have indicated earlier, the alternative strategies are:-

- to accept current strengths but try and use them more extensively

- to build up a style on which a low score has been obtained.

The trainer can suggest that people choose one strategy, or give them the option of choosing either. The important point is that the second strategy requires more time, determination and support. The task set could be 'Using all the information and material now available to you, plan how to improve your capacity to use at least one of the styles'. As we suggested in chapter 5, pairing opposites can be an extremely productive way of helping people to build from low scores.

Learning from learning to learn

It is important to give people the opportunity to review the effectiveness of any plans they have drawn up. If this session forms part of a one or two week course (or longer) then review sessions can be built in. Pairs can repeat their 'be helpful' tasks, and problems and progress reported to the trainer. See also the suggestions in chapter 2.

A timetable

The more extended options presented here will take longer than the 90 minutes outlined in chapter 2. They might be used within a single day, or might be spread over a number of days on a longer programme. As an indication here is a possible timetable, based on Option 2.

Time	Activity	Method	
45 mins	How do we learn	Exercise & discussion	Plenary
45 mins	The task cycle & learning cycle	Talk & discussion	Plenary
90 mins	Learning styles	Description & validity	Plenary + Pairs + Plenary
60 mins	Improving learning styles	An exercise	Pairs + Plenary
45 mins	Using learning styles to help others	Talk & discussion	Plenary
30 mins	Using learning styles to help others	An exercise	Pairs
30 mins	Review of progress	Task	Pairs

A further option

Both in normal working life and on courses the capacity to recognise and use the strengths of others is as important for learning as for many other things. Our colleague Graham Robinson has developed a neat process, in which he asks people with the same predominant learning style to work together in a group in which they design a learning experience for a group with a quite different learning style.

There are two options, or possibly even both can be done, one succeeding the other. For example an Activist group can be asked to prepare an Activist exercise for a group of Reflectors, and a Reflector group to prepare a Reflector exercise for Activists. As a second stage the Activists can be asked to prepare a Reflector exercise for a group of Reflectors. It will be seen that while both exercises stretch the Activists, the second actually requires them to build an additional strength for themselves.

Learning Logs

Some detailed ideas on how and why to use learning logs are given in 'Using Your Learning Styles'. The process of reviewing and reflecting on experience in order to learn better from it is, of course, highly valued by us as trainers (even those of us who are not naturally strong Reflectors!). However, it is not easily accepted by those people for whom it is an unnatural and initially therefore unhelpful process. In Learning to Learn sessions, pause before asking them to do learning logs and ask participants which styles are likely to be most in favour and which most opposed to the idea of the learning log. (Readers of this chapter might similarly like to pause and think about the answer to this.)

One useful route here is to ask people to work in pairs. While a few Activists will pick up the idea of learning logs and work on them during a course, very few will be able to continue this afterwards. However the strong Reflectors, who are more inclined to adapt to this process, can help Activists if they work in pairs. The Reflector can share information he or she has written down and aid the Activist to think through recent experiences. As an alternative to the specially created learning log, which some people find 'unnatural', it is worth asking them to add notes about learning to something they produce anyway. Examples are priority lists, 'to do' lists, filofax planners.

One result of the kind of Learning to Learn process described here could be greater embarrassment for tutors when they are faced by a group who are more knowledgeable about their own learning. If trainers have designed the programme on principles of the learning cycle, and have reviewed the learning preferences of the particular group, then this area of potential conflict is much reduced. A more positive test can be seen through the following:-

On a course

–   Do the participants keep a visible record of their learning styles, refer to them during the programme, and make use of each other's strengths in forming an effective learning group?

On the job

–   Do previous course participants use learning styles information to generate more effective learning from the opportunities they meet or create for themselves?

–   Do they provide more effective learning experiences for others, eg the Activist boss with a Reflector subordinate?

CHAPTER 8

LEARNING ABOUT YOURSELF AS A TRAINER

We have found that many trainers, when they identify their own learning style preferences, realise for the first time how influential those preferences have been in what they offer to others. For example strong Theorists tend to go for highly structured processes supported by models and theories. Activists provide plenty of tasks and simulations.

So the first question for trainers when reviewing their own questionnaire results is 'Am I over using one style in what I offer?' They may then choose to develop themselves, in two dimensions, as trainers and as learners.

As trainers, development may be to cover the learning cycle more effectively and to respond to learners whose style differs from the trainer's preferences.

We strongly advise that trainers not only complete and score the questionnaire for themselves but that they also try the exercises and suggestions contained here and in 'Using Your Learning Styles'. They could tackle first the ideas for using existing preferences. However, we think it essential that trainers should also tackle at least some exercises for building additional strengths, the second strategy we have mentioned earlier. Not only is this a wholly appropriate thing for advisers on learning processes, but we think it essential for them to be able to say that they have attempted (preferably with subsequent success) something which they may recommend to others. (Peter Honey's work on his own development styles of learning is given in the bibliography in chapter 10.)

Your own learning review and learning log

We have mentioned in chapter 7 why the learning review and learning log approach is particularly important, but also why it is difficult. It may be just as difficult for a trainer as it is for anyone else but, it is even more essential. It is generally desirable that trainers should review all aspects of what they do and what they have learned from it - for which the learning log approach is one sensible vehicle. It is especially necessary in relation to using learning styles. Since trainers are engaged in using a theory about learning, some disciplines in relation to it and a particular instrument, it is very important that they record their impressions, what they have learned from using the material, and what ought to be done next time. In other words go round the learning cycle.

Of course beyond that there is the sensible discipline of keeping learning reviews and learning logs in relation to all the activities in which the trainer is involved. Again this is something which is desirable to undertake because it is a process the trainer is likely to recommend to others.

Using others to help

Since many trainers work in conjunction with others, either permanent members of their team or consultants brought in from outside, remember that the strength of other people can help with this process. In the same way that we have recommended the construction and use of groups in learning activities on a course or on the job, so trainers can find help from others. Strong Activists, for example, might well benefit from finding strong Reflector colleagues and using the different ideas available from them. Similarly, Pragmatists normally attracted to immediate utility might learn from the more detached vision of strong Theorists.

Collecting statistical data

We find that some of our most consistent users fail to collect statistical information from their use of the questionnaire. They should collect data on any occasion on which they use it, so that they can create appropriate norms. This will significantly enhance the credibility of the questionnaire for some of the people they advise. We know a number of trainers would not rate the collection of data as one of their preferred activities (especially if they are Activists!) and could have it as one of their 'building' strategies to undertake this task. An alternative is to find a colleague who will do it for them. For example, sometimes the collection of statistical information can be undertaken by an administrator or assistant (ie a non trainer) on a programme, and is something which provides an additional source of interest and satisfaction to them.

We are very interested to have your information, experiences, comments, suggestions. Some can be turned into articles for general circulation, and others can be incorporated in future editions of this Manual. Please send them to Peter Honey at Ardingly House, 10 Linden Avenue, Maidenhead, Berkshire SL6 6HB.

Although this Manual is entirely devoted to learning styles, there are other issues about effective learning.

–   Do individuals have the skills to learn?

–   Does their organisational environment encourage or discourage learning?

–   Are the attitudes and emotions people have facilitating or hindering learning?

These major aspects are covered in our second major tool, the Learning Diagnostic Questionnaire, available in 'The Manual of Learning Opportunities'.

CHAPTER 9

NORMS AND OTHER STATISTICS

This chapter gives basic statistical data for the Learning Styles Questionnaire. Like the remainder of this Manual it is written for a target population of trainers and not for statisticians. It contains more than enough information to help trainers interpret questionnaire results and answer queries that might arise (usually from Theorists!) about the 'respectability' of the instrument. Undoubtedly the most useful data are the tables giving the general norms and norms for different occupational groups. The importance of having comparative data of this kind to assist in the interpretation of the four 'raw' scores was explained in chapter 2.

For trainers who are unfamiliar with statistics, here is a short glossary of statistical terms used in this chapter.

Correlation

A measure indicating the degree of association between two different sets of scores or data eg whether a tendency to cross questionnaire items is associated with a preference for a particular style.

Mean (M)

The sum of all the scores divided by the number of scores.

Norms

Scores broken up into percentile bands without assuming that the scores for a sample of people are normally distributed. The norms in this chapter are expressed in five bands, A the top 10% of scores, B the next 20% of scores, C the middle 40% of scores, D the next 20% of scores, E the lowest 10% of scores.

Reliability

An indication of the extent to which the questionnaire results obtained by a person on one occasion correlate with the results obtained by the same person on another occasion. Reliability is checked by using a test - retest routine.

Standard Deviation (SD)

An indication of the dispersion or variability amongst a set of scores. It is based upon squared deviations from the mean of a set of scores.

Validity

An indication of the extent to which the questionnaire accurately measures what it is designed to measure.

General Norms

General norms for a wide cross section of professional/managerial people working in industry and commerce in the UK.

N = 3500

	Band A	Band B	Band C	Band D	Band E	
Activist	13-20	11-12	7-10 (mean 9.3)	4-6	0-3	SD 2.9
Reflector	18-20	15-17	12-14 (mean 13.6)	9-11	0-8	SD 3.1
Theorist	16-20	14-15	11-13 (mean 12.5)	8-10	0-7	SD 3.2
Pragmatist	17-20	15-16	12-14 (mean 13.7)	9-11	0-8	SD 2.9

Occupational norms

Here, in alphabetical order, are norms for seventeen different occupational groups:-

Norms for 188 Banking Managers (First line)

	Band A	Band B	Band C	Band D	Band E	
Activist	15-20	13-14	9-12 (mean 9.9)	6-8	0-5	SD 3.5
Reflector	18-20	17-17	12-16 (mean 13.2)	9-11	0-8	SD 3.6
Theorist	17-20	15-16	12-14 (mean 12.1)	9-11	0-8	SD 3.0
Pragmatist	18-20	17-17	14-16 (mean 14.1)	11-13	0-10	SD 2.4

Norms for 412 Civil Servants

	Band A	Band B	Band C	Band D	Band E	
Activist	13-20	9-12	6-8 (mean 7.7)	4-5	0-3	SD 3.4
Reflector	18-20	16-17	12-15 (mean 14.0)	9-11	0-8	SD 4.2
Theorist	17-20	15-16	13-14 (mean 13.1)	10-11	0-9	SD 3.2
Pragmatist	16-20	15-15	12-14 (mean 12.7)	9-11	0-8	SD 3.1

Norms for 173 Engineering / Science Graduates

	Band A	Band B	Band C	Band D	Band E	
Activist	13-20	11-12	6-10 (mean 8.6)	4-5	0-3	SD 3.8
Reflector	18-20	16-17	12-15 (mean 14.2)	9-11	0-8	SD 3.6
Theorist	16-20	14-15	11-13 (mean 12.2)	8-10	0-7	SD 3.2
Pragmatist	16-20	14-15	11-13 (mean 12.7)	9-10	0-8	SD 3.0

Norms for 160 Finance Managers

	Band A	Band B	Band C	Band D	Band E	
Activist	10-20	8-9	6-7 (mean 7.0)	3-5	0-2	SD 1.7
Reflector	19-20	16-18	14-15 (mean 14.9)	10-13	0-9	SD 1.6
Theorist	18-20	16-17	13-15 (mean 14.5)	11-12	0-10	SD 2.2
Pragmatist	18-20	16-17	14-15 (mean 15.3)	11-13	0-10	SD 1.4

Norms for 93 Marketing Managers

	Band A	Band B	Band C	Band D	Band E	
Activist	13-20	11-12	7-10 (mean 9.3)	4-6	0-3	SD 2.9
Reflector	18-20	16-17	12-15 (mean 13.8)	9-11	0-8	SD 3.2
Theorist	16-20	14-15	10-13 (mean 12.5)	7-9	0-6	SD 3.4
Pragmatist	17-20	15-16	13-14 (mean 13.6)	10-12	0-9	SD 2.4

Norms for 144 Nurse Tutors

	Band A	Band B	Band C	Band D	Band E	
Activist	16-20	14-15	9-13 (mean 10.5)	6-8	0-5	SD 3.8
Reflector	19-20	17-18	13-16 (mean 13.3)	8-12	0-7	SD 4.3
Theorist	17-20	15-16	9-14 (mean 10.7)	5-8	0-4	SD 4.6
Pragmatist	17-20	15-16	11-14 (mean 11.9)	8-10	0-7	SD 3.5

Norms for 121 Pharmacists / Trainee Pharmacists

	Band A	Band B	Band C	Band D	Band E	
Activist	14-20	11-13	8-10 (mean 8.6)	6-7	0-5	SD 3.2
Reflector	20-20	18-19	15-17 (mean 15.2)	12-14	0-11	SD 3.1
Theorist	17-20	15-16	12-14 (mean 12.4)	9-11	0-8	SD 3.2
Pragmatist	17-20	15-16	12-14 (mean 12.6)	10-11	0-9	SD 3.1

Norms for 176 Police Inspectors

	Band A	Band B	Band C	Band D	Band E	
Activist	15-20	12-14	8-11 (mean 9.3)	6-7	0-5	SD 3.3
Reflector	20-20	18-19	13-17 (mean 14.2)	10-12	0-9	SD 3.5
Theorist	17-20	15-16	12-14 (mean 12.4)	9-11	0-8	SD 3.0
Pragmatist	18-20	16-17	14-15 (mean 13.9)	12-13	0-11	SD 2.6

Norms for 198 Police Sergeants

	Band A	Band B	Band C	Band D	Band E	
Activist	13-20	10-12	7-9 (mean 8.1)	6-6	0-5	SD 2.8
Reflector	18-20	17-17	14-16 (mean 14.2)	12-13	0-11	SD 3.0
Theorist	18-20	15-17	12-14 (mean 12.6)	10-11	0-9	SD 3.1
Pragmatist	17-20	15-16	12-14 (mean 12.5)	10-11	0-9	SD 2.8

Norms for 178 Production Managers

	Band A	Band B	Band C	Band D	Band E	
Activist	12-20	9-11	6-8 (mean 7.4)	3-5	0-2	SD 3.4
Reflector	17-20	15-16	11-14 (mean 12.7)	7-10	0-6	SD 4.0
Theorist	19-20	17-18	14-16 (mean 15.2)	12-13	0-11	SD 1.3
Pragmatist	19-20	17-18	15-16 (mean 16.0)	12-14	0-11	SD 1.9

Norms for 262 Research and Development Managers

	Band A	Band B	Band C	Band D	Band E	
Activist	13-20	10-12	6-9 (mean 8.0)	4-5	0-3	SD 3.4
Reflector	18-20	16-17	13-15 (mean 14.5)	10-12	0-9	SD 3.0
Theorist	17-20	15-16	12-14 (mean 13.1)	9-11	0-8	SD 2.8
Pragmatist	17-20	15-16	12-14 (mean 13.4)	9-11	0-8	SD 2.8

Norms for 189 Salespersons

	Band A	Band B	Band C	Band D	Band E	
Activist	17-20	15-16	12-14 (mean 13.3)	9-11	0-8	SD 2.9
Reflector	15-20	12-14	10-11 (mean 11.5)	7-9	0-6	SD 2.8
Theorist	17-20	14-16	9-13 (mean 11.4)	6-8	0-5	SD 3.6
Pragmatist	18-20	16-17	13-15 (mean 14.1)	10-12	0-9	SD 3.0

Norms for 374 6th Form Teachers / Lecturers

	Band A	Band B	Band C	Band D	Band E	
Activist	15-20	12-14	7-11 (mean 8.7)	5-6	0-4	SD 3.9
Reflector	19-20	17-18	13-16 (mean 13.9)	10-12	0-9	SD 3.7
Theorist	18-20	15-17	12-14 (mean 12.4)	9-11	0-8	SD 3.3
Pragmatist	17-20	15-16	13-14 (mean 12.5)	10-12	0-9	SD 3.0

Norms for 165 Students (A Level / Diploma)

	Band A	Band B	Band C	Band D	Band E	
Activist	17-20	15-16	10-14 (mean 11.1)	7-9	0-6	SD 3.8
Reflector	19-20	17-18	13-16 (mean 13.7)	10-12	0-9	SD 3.8
Theorist	16-20	14-15	9-13 (mean 10.2)	6-8	0-5	SD 3.8
Pragmatist	16-20	14-15	10-13 (mean 11.2)	8-9	0-7	SD 3.2

Norms for 189 Student Nurses (1st, 2nd, and 3rd year)

	Band A	Band B	Band C	Band D	Band E	
Activist	16-20	13-15	9-12 (mean 10.3)	6-8	0-5	SD 3.8
Reflector	19-20	18-18	14-17 (mean 14.3)	10-13	0-9	SD 3.4
Theorist	17-20	15-16	12-14 (mean 12.1)	9-11	0-8	SD 2.8
Pragmatist	17-20	15-16	12-14 (mean 12.7)	10-11	0-9	SD 2.6

Norms for 148 Supervisors

	Band A	Band B	Band C	Band D	Band E	
Activist	16-20	12-15	8-11 (mean 9.7)	6-7	0-5	SD 3.6
Reflector	19-20	17-18	14-16 (mean 14.6)	11-13	0-10	SD 3.2
Theorist	17-20	15-16	11-14 (mean 12.2)	9-10	0-8	SD 3.0
Pragmatist	18-20	16-17	13-15 (mean 13.1)	11-12	0-10	SD 2.7

Norms for 194 Trainers

	Band A	Band B	Band C	Band D	Band E	
Activist	16-20	14-15	9-13 (mean 10.4)	7-8	0-6	SD 3.7
Reflector	19-20	16-18	12-15 (mean 12.4)	8-11	0-7	SD 4.1
Theorist	17-20	15-16	11-14 (mean 11.7)	7-10	0-6	SD 3.5
Pragmatist	17-20	16-16	12-15 (mean 12.9)	10-11	0-9	SD 3.0

Comparisons of occupational norms

The following scattergram gives a pictorial summary based on a comparison of the means for all the occupations. Occupations nearest the point where the axes cross have the most 'balanced' learning style preferences, eg Civil Servants, Police Inspectors and Marketing Managers. The further occupations are away from the midpoint the more it indicates strong preferences and a lack of 'balance', eg Salespersons have strong Activist/Pragmatist preferences, Production Managers have strong Theorist/Pragmatist preferences, Finance Managers have strong Theorist preferences.

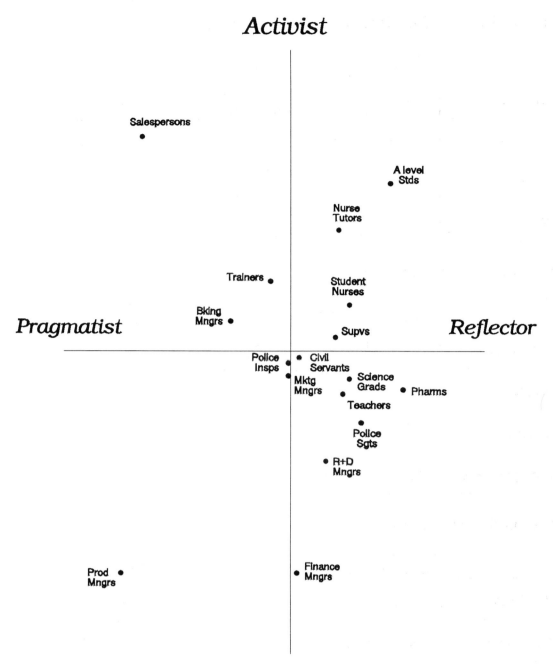

Activist

Salespersons
•

A level
• Stds

Nurse
Tutors
•

Trainers •

Student
Nurses
•

Pragmatist

Bking
Mngrs •

• Supvs

Reflector

Police
Insps •
• Civil
Servants

Mktg
Mngrs •
• Science
Grads

• Pharms

Teachers
•

Police
Sgts
•

• R+D
Mngrs

Prod •
Mngrs

Finance
• Mngrs

Theorist

Gender norms

Here are norms for random samples of males and females. Both samples were drawn from comparable populations of professional people and junior management from a cross-section of occupations in commerce/industry. People often wonder if there are significant gender differences in learning style preferences and these norms seem to suggest not.

The means show women to be slightly more Activist than men (perhaps because they have to be!) and men to have slightly stronger preferences for Theorist and Pragmatist.

Norms for 117 Females

	Band A	Band B	Band C	Band D	Band E	
Activist	15-20	12-14	8-11 (mean 9.6)	6-7	0-5	SD 3.4
Reflector	19-20	16-18	12-15 (mean 12.9)	8-11	0-7	SD 3.8
Theorist	17-20	15-16	12-14 (mean 12.0)	9-11	0-8	SD 2.9
Pragmatist	17-20	15-16	12-14 (mean 13.0)	11-11	0-10	SD 2.5

Norms for 117 Males

	Band A	Band B	Band C	Band D	Band E	
Activist	15-20	12-14	8-11 (mean 9.0)	6-7	0-5	SD 3.5
Reflector	19-20	17-18	12-16 (mean 12.9)	8-11	0-7	SD 4.1
Theorist	17-20	16-16	12-15 (mean 12.5)	9-11	0-8	SD 3.1
Pragmatist	18-20	17-17	14-16 (mean 13.6)	10-13	0-9	SD 3.1

Cultural comparisons

The questionnaire has been translated into French, German, Spanish, Portuguese and Swedish, but we have no data about results obtained in those countries.

The information from other countries is:-

	USA N = 862	Canada N = 46	Greece/Fem N = 228	Greece/Male N = 342
Activist	Mean 9.9	Mean 8.5	Mean 12.5	Mean 11.0
Reflector	Mean 13.2	Mean 13.9	Mean 15.8	Mean 16.4
Theorist	Mean 12.8	Mean 13.6	Mean 12.4	Mean 14.1
Pragmatist	Mean 13.1	Mean 14.0	Mean 11.4	Mean 13.1

In addition we are grateful to Neil Habershon for supplying the following data compiled from the results of 365 managers attending the IBM Executive Management School. A shortened version of the questionnaire was used (see the references to The Guardian article) and so the IBM data have been adjusted to make them comparable with the means already given in this chapter.

	France N = 51	Ger/Aus N = 53	Italy N = 28	Scand. N = 44	Switz N = 34	UK/Ire N = 34	USA N = 32
Activist	10.7	9.9	10.9	12.1	11.8	12.0	11.5
Reflector	11.7	10.8	12.0	9.9	11.7	9.3	10.4
Theorist	12.7	11.3	13.7	9.9	11.7	10.7	11.8
Pragmatist	14.3	13.5	14.1	13.1	14.8	13.3	13.9

These means plotted on a scattergram give the following picture:-

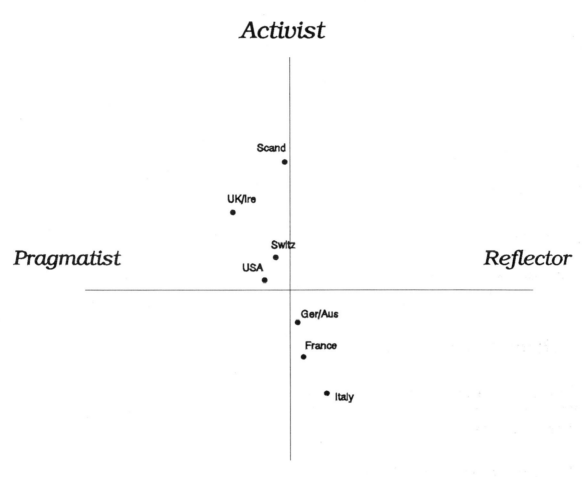

Reliability

Reliability is high for an instrument of this kind. The consistency, or reliability of the questionnaire was checked by getting a total of 50 people to complete the questionnaire twice, with a two week gap between the two occasions. The correlation (Pearson's product-moment coefficient of correlation) between the two sets of results was a very satisfactory 0.89. People with strong Theorist and Reflector preferences were the most consistent with correlations of 0.95 and 0.92 respectively. Pragmatists produce a test-retest consistency of 0.87, and Activists were the least consistent with a correlation of 0.81.

D K Wilson of Sunderland Business School also found high reliability with test-retest results ranging from 0.80 for Reflectors to 0.86 for Activists (see bibliography).

Validity

Face validity (as opposed to real validity) for the questionnaire is not in doubt. It has been rare for us to encounter anyone who disputes the accuracy of their questionnaire result. (See chapter 2.)

The technical validity of the questionnaire is harder to determine especially in the area where there are few established questionnaires with which to draw comparisons. (See Hayes in bibliography for some views.) One of the authors has checked its validity on courses by making specific behavioural predictions (such as those listed in chapters 3 and 4). The predictions have been found to be largely accurate but this hardly constitutes a respectable proof of validity.

The amount of overlap between the four learning styles

The correlations are:-

	Activist	Reflector	Theorist	Pragmatist
Activist	x	-0.013	0.097	0.299
Reflector	-0.013	x	0.71	0.42
Theorist	0.097	0.71	x	0.54
Pragmatist	0.299	0.42	0.54	x

This shows that, in descending order of likelihood, the most common combinations are:-

      1st   Reflector/Theorist

      2nd   Theorist/Pragmatist

      3rd   Reflector/Pragmatist

      4th   Activist/Pragmatist

The other two combinations (Activist/Reflector and Activist/Theorist) are less likely to occur since in both cases the correlation between them is virtually zero.

Dominant Styles

We have done a sampling exercise to find the extent to which people are dominated by one style, rather than being all round learners. The results sustain our basic proposition; that learners often have a strong preference for one or two learning styles. Strong is defined as bands A and B in the norms ie the top 30% of scores.

Random sample of 300 managers:-

With one strong preference	35%
With two strong preferences	24%
With three strong preferences	20%
With four strong preferences	2%
With no strong preferences	19%

The significance of questionnaire items ticked and crossed

We have analysed a random sample of 100 completed questionnaires to discover ticking and crossing patterns. As the results below show, a few items in the questionnaire are ticked by 90% or more people. Obviously these items are failing to discriminate adequately and could therefore be excluded. We would, however, prefer to retain them because they provide a more complete picture of each learning style.

Activist		Reflector		Theorist		Pragmatist	
LSQ item	% who ticked	LSQ item	% who ticked	LSQ item	% who ticked	LSQ item	% who ticked
2	36	7	48	1	82	5	68
4	52	13	79	3	88	9	95
6	55	15	81	8	80	11	72
10	76	16	85	12	44	19	86
17	29	25	33	14	63	21	86
23	94	28	76	18	83	27	84
24	84	29	68	20	87	35	56
32	64	31	67	22	19	37	86
34	42	33	70	26	34	44	90
38	15	36	33	30	61	49	79
40	37	39	55	42	55	50	95
43	30	41	67	47	89	53	85
45	19	46	75	51	87	54	83
48	28	52	85	57	92	56	93
58	29	55	44	61	54	59	77
64	50	60	67	63	92	65	31
71	19	62	48	68	72	69	60
72	15	66	91	75	75	70	37
74	36	67	56	77	78	73	67
79	80	76	89	78	44	80	30

Summing the four scores for Activist, Reflector, Theorist and Pragmatist we have found that the lowest combined score so far encountered is 22 and the highest 59 with a mean, for the whole population tested so far, of 48.6 and standard deviation of 8.2. We were naturally curious to see if a high or low combined score was particularly associated with any of the learning styles. In fact there are some very significant trends. The correlations between style preferences and high or low combined scores are as follows:-

Theorist	0.90
Reflector	0.80
Pragmatist	0.74
Activist	0.48

These correlations indicate a particularly strong association between the Theorist style and the tendency to be a high or low ticker of the questionnaire items. In other words a person with a strong Theorist style is likely to have a high combined score (ie ticked lots of items) and conversely, a person with a low Theorist style is likely to have a low combined score (ie crossed lots of items).

Shorter version of the Learning Styles Questionnaire

Although the shorter IBM version produces quicker and an apparently equivalent 'result' we believe the larger number of questions produces a better development vehicle.

Norm calculating service

If trainers wish to have norms calculated for special occupational groups, send Peter Honey a note of the four raw scores obtained by forty plus people, with a clear indication of their occupational grouping. There will be a nominal charge of approximately £50 for this service depending on the volume of data to be processed. A firm quotation will be given before proceeding.

CHAPTER 10

LITERATURE ON LEARNING STYLES

We have divided our review of the literature into four sections:-

1.   Prime additional reading for the busy trainer.

2.   Additional articles and books by ourselves on learning styles.

3.   A bibliography of work by others on our learning styles.

4.   Related material.

Section 1:   Prime additional reading for the busy trainer

Any selection is invidious, but the following (in alphabetical order) are particularly helpful:-

Boak G	'Managerial Competencies: The Management Learning Contract Approach', Pitman, 1991
Butler J	'Learning Design for Effective Executive Programmes' in 'Handbook of Management Development', Third Edition edited by Alan Mumford, Gower, 1991
Caiae B	'Learning in Style - Reflection on an Action Learning MBA Programme', Journal of Management Development, Vol. 6, No. 2, 1987
Honey P	'Styles of Learning' in 'Handbook of Management Development', Third Edition, edited by Alan Mumford, Gower, 1991
Mumford A	'Making a Career Through Learning', International Journal of Career Management, Vol. 2, No. 1, 1990
Seymour R & West-Burnham J	'Learning Styles and Education Management', International Journal of Education Management, Part one: Vol. 3, No. 4, 1989; Part two: Vol. 4, No. 4, 1990

The major theoretical work which, of course, explains his own version of learning styles is:-

Kolb D	'Experiential Learning', Prentice Hall, 1984

Section 2: Honey/Mumford articles/books on learning styles

We have listed our own articles in chronological order.

1. Honey P   'Learning Styles - their relevance to Training Courses', Training Officer, April 1983

2. Honey P   'Learning Styles and Self Development', Training & Development, January 1984

3. Honey P & Povah N   'Self Development: Overcoming the Paradox', Industrial & Commercial Training, July/August 1986

4. Honey P & Lobley R   'Learning from Outdoor Activities: Getting the Balance Right', Industrial & Commercial Training, Nov/Dec 1986

5. Honey P   'The Iterative Secret', Management Education and Development, Vol. 18 Pt.1, 1987

6. Honey P   'You Are What You Learn', Nursing Times, Vol. 84, No. 36, 1988

7. Honey P   'Trials & Tribulations', The Guardian, 19.12.1989

8. Honey P   'Confessions of a Learner', Training & Development, May 1990

9. Honey P   'Styles of Learning', in 'Handbook of Management Development', Third Edition, edited by Alan Mumford, Gower, 1991

10. Mumford A   'Learning Styles and Learning Skills', Journal of Management Development, Vol. 1, No. 2, 1982

11. Mumford A   'The Influence of Learning Styles on Learning', Training and Development in Australia, Vol. 13, No. 1, 1986

12. Mumford A   'Learning to Learn for Managers', Journal of European Industrial Training, Vol. 10, No. 2, 1986

13. Mumford A   'Learning to Learn for Managers: Literature Review', Management Bibliographies and Reviews, Vol. 1, No. 2, 1986

14. Mumford A   'Self Development: Missing Elements', Industrial & Commercial Training, May/June 1986

15. Mumford A & Honey P   'Developing Skills for Matrix Management', Industrial & Commercial Training, September/October 1986

16. Mumford A   'Learning Styles and Learning', Personnel Review, Vol. 16, No. 3, 1987

17. Mumford A   'Helping Managers Learn to Learn', Journal of Management Development, Vol. 6, No. 5, 1987

18. Mumford A   'Helping the Individual Learn', Banking and Financial Training, Vol. 3, No. 3, 1987

19.	Mumford A	'Learning to Learn and Managing Self Development', in 'Applying Self Development in Organisations', edited by M Pedlar, J Burgoyne and T Boydell, Prentice Hall, 1988
20.	Mumford A	'Management Development: Strategies for Action', Institute of Personnel Management, 1989
21.	Mumford A	'The Individual and Learning Opportunities', Industrial and Commercial Training, Vol. 22, No. 1, January 1990
22.	Mumford A	'Making a Career Through Learning', International Journal of Career Management, Vol. 2, No. 1, 1990
23.	Mumford A	'Learning Styles Epitaphs', Management Education and Development, Vol. 22, Part 1, 1991
24.	Mumford A	'How Women Managers Learn', Women In Management Newsletter, Summer 1991
25.	Mumford A	'Women Managers as Learners', E W M D News, Issue 29, Autumn 1991

Section 3: A bibliography of work by others on our learning styles

1.	Allinson C W & Hayes J	'The Learning Styles Questionnaire: An Alternative to Kolb's Inventory?' Journal of Management Studies, Vol. 25, No. 3, 1988
2.	Barrett P	'The Learning Community', Industrial & Commercial Training, March/April 1986
3.	Binsted D	'Issues in Management Development', Centre for Study in Management Learning, 1985
4.	Binsted D	'Design for Learning', in Journal of European Industrial Training, Vol. 4, No. 8, 1980
5.	Boak G	'Managerial Competencies: The Management Learning Contract Approach', Pitman, 1991
6.	Butler J	'Learning More Effectively on a General Management Programme', Industrial & Commercial Training, July/August 1988
7.	Butler J	'Learning Design for Effective Executive Programmes', in 'Handbook of Management Development', Third Edition, edited by Alan Mumford, Gower, 1991
8.	Caiae B	'Learning in Style - Reflection of an Action Learning MBA Programme', Journal of Management Development, Vol. 6, No. 2, 1987
9.	Canning R	'Management Self Development' Journal of European Industrial Training, Vol. 8, No. 1, 1984
10.	Carter G	'Learning Styles and Team Behaviour', M Psych Thesis for University of Queensland, 1988

11. Carter G — 'A Strategy for Cost Effective Training and Development', Training & Development in Australia, Vol. 15, No. 1, 1988

12. Coates J — 'How People Learn on Management Courses', Industrial & Commercial Training, March/April 1988

13. Corder C — 'Teaching Hard, Teaching Soft', Gower, 1990

14. Delahaye B & Thompson B — 'Learning Styles - What Do They Measure?' Asia Pacific Human Resource Management, Winter 1991

15. Downing F G — 'When an Activist is asked to Reflect Theologically - or any other way', British Journal of Theological Education, Vol. 3, No. 2, 1990

16. Harrison R — 'Training and Development', IPM, 1988

17. Hayes J & Allinson C W — 'Cultural Differences in the Learning Styles of Managers', Management International Review, Vol. 28, No. 3, 1988

18. Hinton I — 'Learning to Manage and Managing to Learn', Industrial & Commercial Training, May/June 1984

19. Keal P — 'A New Style in Burton: Learning', Industrial & Commercial Training, May/June 1988

20. Kendall R — 'Internalising Learning for Self Development', Industrial and Commercial Training, November/December 1987

21. Lewis A & Bolden K J — 'General Practitioners and their Learning Styles', Journal of the Royal College of General Practitioners, May 1989

22. MacArthur J — 'Learning to Learn in a Work Situation', Executive Development, Vol. 4, No. 4, 1991

23. Margerison C — 'Making Management Development Work', McGraw-Hill, 1991

24. Middleton J — 'How Trainees Learn', Horizons, July 1990

25. Pont T — 'Developing Effective Training Skills', McGraw-Hill, 1991

26. Rae L — 'The Application of Learning Styles', Industrial & Commercial Training, March/April 1986

27. Rushby N — 'Accommodating Individual Learning Styles', Personnel Management, October 1988

28. Scriven R — 'Learning Circles', Journal of European Industrial Training, Vol. 8, No. 1, 1984

29. Seymour R & West-Burnham J — 'Learning Styles and Education Management', International Journal of Education Management, Part one: Vol. 3, No. 4, 1989; Part two: Vol. 4, No. 4, 1990

30.	Walmsley P	'Using the Learning Styles Questionnaire', Industrial & Commercial Training, Vol. 23, No. 1, 1991
31.	Wicks A	'Use of Learning Styles Questionnaire', Industrial & Commercial Training, November/December 1989
32.	Wicks A	'Learning Styles and Distance Educators', Industrial & Commercial Training, Vol. 23, No. 5, 1991
33.	Williams T	'Repertory Grid combined with Learning Styles', Industrial & Commercial Training, March/April 1987
34.	Wilson D K	'Management Learning', PhD Thesis for University of Lancaster, 1989
35.	Wood S (Editor)	'Continuous Development', IPM, 1988

Section 4:   Related Honey/Mumford Materials

Using Your Learning Styles

As indicated earlier, the Learning Styles Questionnaire can be used both to improve the design of learning experiences for groups and individuals, and also as a first step towards helping individuals learn how to learn more effectively. For this latter purpose the personal workbook 'Using Your Learning Styles' is a primary resource. Since it is fundamental that the individual learner should have the opportunity to use better the learning strengths already possessed, and preferably develop additional strengths, this is an important adjunct to this Manual.

USA version

The Manual of Learning Styles and Using Your Learning Styles are available in a slightly different format from:-

> Organization Design and Development
> 2002 Renaissance Boulevard,
> Suite 100,   King of Prussia,   PA 19406,   USA

Foreign language versions

The Manual and accompanying document have also been published for use in Scandinavia by:-

> Utbildningshuset
> Studentlitteratur
> Box 141,   S-221 00 Lund,   Sweden

The questionnaire and general descriptions have been translated into French, German, Spanish and Portuguese. Copies of these translations can be obtained from Peter Honey provided that the prospective purchasers already have the Manual in English.

Software version

A floppy disc containing the questionnaire and scoring/interpreting routines is available from:

Corporate Assessment Network Limited
44 Sheen Lane,
East Sheen,
London SW14 8LG

Tel: 081 392 9118

Shortened versions

We have commented in chapter 9 on the validity and reliability of the questionnaire, which clearly applies only to managerial and professional people. (In this sense it differs from Kolb's LSI.) We know that several people have experimented with alternative versions, using the same principles, for young people. We would be very interested to hear of such versions. Alan Mumford in working with Young Enterprise has produced a version appropriate to 16-19 year old school children, using different questions and different descriptions, but the same principles.

In December 1989 a shortened version of the questionnaire appeared in The Guardian (see bibliography). We commented in the previous chapter on our reasons for preferring our full version.

LEARNING STYLES QUESTIONNAIRE   revised 1986

This questionnaire is designed to find out your preferred learning style(s). Over the years you have probably developed learning 'habits' that help you benefit more from some experiences than from others. Since you are probably unaware of this, this questionnaire will help you pinpoint your learning preferences so that you are in a better position to select learning experiences that suit your style.

There is no time limit to this questionnaire. It will probably take you 10-15 minutes. The accuracy of the results depends on how honest you can be. There are no right or wrong answers. If you agree more than you disagree with a statement put a tick by it (✓). If you disagree more than you agree put a cross by it (x). Be sure to mark each item with either a tick or cross.

- [ ] 1. I have strong beliefs about what is right and wrong, good and bad.

- [ ] 2. I often act without considering the possible consequences.

- [ ] 3. I tend to solve problems using a step-by-step approach.

- [ ] 4. I believe that formal procedures and policies restrict people.

- [ ] 5. I have a reputation for saying what I think, simply and directly.

- [ ] 6. I often find that actions based on feelings are as sound as those based on careful thought and analysis.

- [ ] 7. I like the sort of work where I have time for thorough preparation and implementation.

- [ ] 8. I regularly question people about their basic assumptions.

- [ ] 9. What matters most is whether something works in practice.

- [ ] 10. I actively seek out new experiences.

- [ ] 11. When I hear about a new idea or approach I immediately start working out how to apply it in practice.

- [ ] 12. I am keen on self discipline such as watching my diet, taking regular exercise, sticking to a fixed routine, etc.

- [ ] 13. I take pride in doing a thorough job.

- [ ] 14. I get on best with logical, analytical people and less well with spontaneous, 'irrational' people.

- [ ] 15. I take care over the interpretation of data available to me and avoid jumping to conclusions.

- [ ] 16. I like to reach a decision carefully after weighing up many alternatives.

- [ ] 17. I'm attracted more to novel, unusual ideas than to practical ones.

- [ ] 18. I don't like disorganised things and prefer to fit things into a coherent pattern.

- [ ] 19. I accept and stick to laid down procedures and policies so long as I regard them as an efficient way of getting the job done.

- [ ] 20. I like to relate my actions to a general principle.

- [ ] 21. In discussions I like to get straight to the point.

☐ 22. I tend to have distant, rather formal relationships with people at work.

☐ 23. I thrive on the challenge of tackling something new and different.

☐ 24. I enjoy fun-loving, spontaneous people.

☐ 25. I pay meticulous attention to detail before coming to a conclusion.

☐ 26. I find it difficult to produce ideas on impulse.

☐ 27. I believe in coming to the point immediately.

☐ 28. I am careful not to jump to conclusions too quickly.

☐ 29. I prefer to have as many sources of information as possible - the more data to think over the better.

☐ 30. Flippant people who don't take things seriously enough usually irritate me.

☐ 31. I listen to other people's points of view before putting my own forward.

☐ 32. I tend to be open about how I'm feeling.

☐ 33. In discussions I enjoy watching the manoeuvrings of the other participants.

☐ 34. I prefer to respond to events on a spontaneous, flexible basis rather than plan things out in advance.

☐ 35. I tend to be attracted to techniques such as network analysis, flow charts, branching programmes, contingency planning, etc.

☐ 36. It worries me if I have to rush out a piece of work to meet a tight deadline.

☐ 37. I tend to judge people's ideas on their practical merits.

☐ 38. Quiet, thoughtful people tend to make me feel uneasy.

☐ 39. I often get irritated by people who want to rush things.

☐ 40. It is more important to enjoy the present moment than to think about the past or future.

☐ 41. I think that decisions based on a thorough analysis of all the information are sounder than those based on intuition.

☐ 42. I tend to be a perfectionist.

☐ 43. In discussions I usually produce lots of spontaneous ideas.

☐ 44. In meetings I put forward practical, realistic ideas.

☐ 45. More often than not, rules are there to be broken.

☐ 46. I prefer to stand back from a situation and consider all the perspectives.

☐ 47. I can often see inconsistencies and weaknesses in other people's arguments.

☐ 48. On balance I talk more than I listen.

☐ 49. I can often see better, more practical ways to get things done.

☐ 50. I think written reports should be short and to the point.

☐ 51. I believe that rational, logical thinking should win the day.

- [ ] 52. I tend to discuss specific things with people rather than engaging in social discussion.

- [ ] 53. I like people who approach things realistically rather than theoretically.

- [ ] 54. In discussions I get impatient with irrelevancies and digressions.

- [ ] 55. If I have a report to write I tend to produce lots of drafts before settling on the final version.

- [ ] 56. I am keen to try things out to see if they work in practice.

- [ ] 57. I am keen to reach answers via a logical approach.

- [ ] 58. I enjoy being the one that talks a lot.

- [ ] 59. In discussions I often find I am the realist, keeping people to the point and avoiding wild speculations.

- [ ] 60. I like to ponder many alternatives before making up my mind.

- [ ] 61. In discussions with people I often find I am the most dispassionate and objective.

- [ ] 62. In discussions I'm more likely to adopt a 'low profile' than to take the lead and do most of the talking.

- [ ] 63. I like to be able to relate current actions to a longer term bigger picture.

- [ ] 64. When things go wrong I am happy to shrug it off and 'put it down to experience'.

- [ ] 65. I tend to reject wild, spontaneous ideas as being impractical.

- [ ] 66. It's best to think carefully before taking action.

- [ ] 67. On balance I do the listening rather than the talking.

- [ ] 68. I tend to be tough on people who find it difficult to adopt a logical approach.

- [ ] 69. Most times I believe the end justifies the means.

- [ ] 70. I don't mind hurting people's feelings so long as the job gets done.

- [ ] 71. I find the formality of having specific objectives and plans stifling.

- [ ] 72. I'm usually one of the people who puts life into a party.

- [ ] 73. I do whatever is expedient to get the job done.

- [ ] 74. I quickly get bored with methodical, detailed work.

- [ ] 75. I am keen on exploring the basic assumptions, principles and theories underpinning things and events.

- [ ] 76. I'm always interested to find out what people think.

- [ ] 77. I like meetings to be run on methodical lines, sticking to laid down agenda, etc.

- [ ] 78. I steer clear of subjective or ambiguous topics.

- [ ] 79. I enjoy the drama and excitement of a crisis situation.

- [ ] 80. People often find me insensitive to their feelings.

LEARNING STYLES - GENERAL DESCRIPTIONS

Activists

Activists involve themselves fully and without bias in new experiences. They enjoy the here and now and are happy to be dominated by immediate experiences. They are open-minded, not sceptical, and this tends to make them enthusiastic about anything new. Their philosophy is: 'I'll try anything once'. They tend to act first and consider the consequences afterwards. Their days are filled with activity. They tackle problems by brainstorming. As soon as the excitement from one activity has died down they are busy looking for the next. They tend to thrive on the challenge of new experiences but are bored with implementation and longer term consolidation. They are gregarious people constantly involving themselves with others but, in doing so, they seek to centre all activities around themselves.

Reflectors

Reflectors like to stand back to ponder experiences and observe them from many different perspectives. They collect data, both first hand and from others, and prefer to think about it thoroughly before coming to any conclusion. The thorough collection and analysis of data about experiences and events is what counts so they tend to postpone reaching definitive conclusions for as long as possible. Their philosophy is to be cautious. They are thoughtful people who like to consider all possible angles and implications before making a move. They prefer to take a back seat in meetings and discussions. They enjoy observing other people in action. They listen to others and get the drift of the discussion before making their own points. They tend to adopt a low profile and have a slightly distant, tolerant unruffled air about them. When they act it is part of a wide picture which includes the past as well as the present and others' observations as well as their own.

Theorists

Theorists adapt and integrate observations into complex but logically sound theories. They think problems through in a vertical, step-by-step logical way. They assimilate disparate facts into coherent theories. They tend to be perfectionists who won't rest easy until things are tidy and fit into a rational scheme. They like to analyze and synthesize. They are keen on basic assumptions, principles, theories models and systems thinking. Their philosophy prizes rationality and logic. 'If it's logical it's good'. Questions they frequently ask are: 'Does it make sense?' 'How does this fit with that?' 'What are the basic assumptions?' They tend to be detached, analytical and dedicated to rational objectivity rather than anything subjective or ambiguous. Their approach to problems is consistently logical. This is their 'mental set' and they rigidly reject anything that doesn't fit with it. They prefer to maximize certainty and feel uncomfortable with subjective judgements, lateral thinking and anything flippant.

Pragmatists

Pragmatists are keen on trying out ideas, theories and techniques to see if they work in practice. They positively search out new ideas and take the first opportunity to experiment with applications. They are the sort of people who return from management courses brimming with new ideas that they want to try out in practice. They like to get on with things and act quickly and confidently on ideas that attract them. They tend to be impatient with ruminating and open-ended discussions. They are essentially practical, down to earth people who like making practical decisions and solving problems. They respond to problems and opportunities 'as a challenge'. Their philosophy is: 'There is always a better way' and 'If it *works* it's good'.

LEARNING STYLES QUESTIONNAIRE – SCORING

You score one point for each item you ticked (✓). There are no points for items you crossed (✗).

Simply indicate on the lists below which items were ticked.

2	7	1	5
4	13	3	9
6	15	8	11
10	16	12	19
17	25	14	21
23	28	18	27
24	29	20	35
32	31	22	37
34	33	26	44
38	36	30	49
40	39	42	50
43	41	47	53
45	46	51	54
48	52	57	56
58	55	61	59
64	60	63	65
71	62	68	69
72	66	75	70
74	67	77	73
79	76	78	80

Totals

Activist	_Reflector_	_Theorist_	_Pragmatist_

Ring your scores on this chart and join up.

Activist	Reflector	Theorist	Pragmatist	
20	20	20	20	
19				
18		19		
17			19	
16	19	18		Very strong preference
15			18	
14		17		
13	18	16	17	
12	17	15	16	
	16			Strong preference
11	15	14	15	
10	14	13	14	
9				
8	13	12	13	Moderate preference
7	12	11	12	
6	11	10	11	
5	10	9	10	Low preference
4	9	8	9	
3	8	7	8	
	7	6	7	
	6	5	6	
2	5	4	5	
	4		4	
	3	3	3	Very low preference
1	2	2	2	
	1	1	1	
0	0	0	0	

Honey and Mumford 1992

LEARNING STYLES QUESTIONNAIRE – SCORING

You score one point for each item you ticked (✓). There are no points for items you crossed (✗).

Simply indicate on the lists below which items were ticked.

2	7	1	5
4	13	3	9
6	15	8	11
10	16	12	19
17	25	14	21
23	28	18	27
24	29	20	35
32	31	22	37
34	33	26	44
38	36	30	49
40	39	42	50
43	41	47	53
45	46	51	54
48	52	57	56
58	55	61	59
64	60	63	65
71	62	68	69
72	66	75	70
74	67	77	73
79	76	78	80

Totals

_____   _____   _____   _____

Activist   *Reflector*   *Theorist*   *Pragmatist*

Plot the scores on the arms of the cross below and apply the appropriate norms from Section 1 (pages 3-10) in the booklet "Using Your Learning Styles".

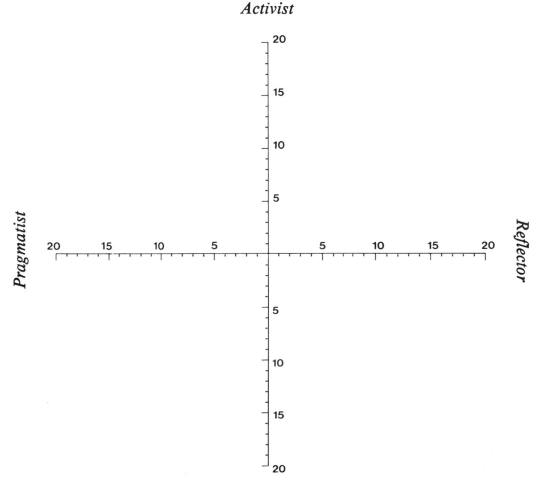

Activist

Pragmatist

Reflector

Theorist

© Honey and Mumford 1986